Here's to Studley, my husband, the bold Ken McKay.

We are paired like a steak with a fine cabernet.

Also by Elaine Ambrose

Menopause Sucks – with Joanne Kimes
Drinking with Dead Women Writers – with AK Turner
Drinking with Dead Drunks – with AK Turner
The Red Tease – A Woman's Adventures in Golf
Gators & Taters – A Week of Bedtime Stories
The Magic Potato – La Papa Mágica
Waiting for the Harvest

Elaine's Short Stories and Poems
Appear in the Following Anthologies

Faith, Hope & Healing – Dr. Bernie Siegel - Wiley
A Miracle Under the Christmas Tree – Harlequin
The Dog with the Old Soul – Harlequin
Hauntings from the Snake River Plain – Other Bunch Press
Tales from the Attic – The Cabin
Beyond Burlap – Junior League of Boise
Daily Erotica - 366 Poems of Passion – Mill Park Publishing
Little White Dress – Mill Park Publishing

~

Elaine Ambrose is available for speaking engagements,
writers' conferences, workshop facilitation, and enthusiastic,
clever conversation. Visit her web site at ElaineAmbrose.com
for all the delightful details. Hurry because she's
not getting any younger.

Midlife Cabernet

life, love & laughter after fifty

Elaine Ambrose

Mill Park Publishing
www.MillParkPublishing.com

Eagle, Idaho

Text copyright ©2014 by Elaine Ambrose
Book cover and design by Sarah Tregay
Author photo by Sherry Briscoe

ISBN: 978-0-9883980-7-8
Printed in USA

Mill Park Publishing
Eagle, ID 83616

Mill Park Publishing
www.MillParkPublishing.com

Contents

Going Under and Beyond the Knife

I never intended to be divorced in my forties, but it happened. And then once again in my fifties. If love is blind, then I need a white cane instead of a white dress. My empty wedding dresses hang useless and unfulfilled as bittersweet symbols of inflated hope that fizzled after tying the knot too loose. Instead of sashaying down the aisle to wedding bliss, I detoured over to Malfunction Junction. I could imagine the sleeves of these dresses slapping me in the face while some mysterious voice mocked, "You're a loser in the love department."

But I wasn't ready to be shoved to the sidelines of life with a group of lonely women—the ones you see on cruises who have to pay the cabin boy to dance with them. Or, the ones who read the obituaries to find eligible widowers and bring them a pot roast and a pie—under low lighting, of course. Or, the ones who wear bright red lipstick and wrap yards of scarves around their necks to hide the wrinkles. And I wasn't ready to stay at home doing laundry just so I could lean against the washing machine during the sexy spin cycle. No, I refused to go there…not yet.

So I sat down with a carafe of fine wine and a plate of cookies and began to study my options for self-improvement by using two columns to describe myself: the *Aged but Adequate* and the *Old and Ornery*. For the positive features, I listed that I could speak in complete sentences, I raised independent, successful children, I could turn over without needing a forklift, and I had the ability to write with both hands while singing in Latin. (I've earned free drinks in bars with that nifty trick.) What man could resist all those attributes?

Alas! The bad qualities were hideous: I snored like a drunken bear with severe allergies, the excess skin on my body was sagging south faster than my industrial-strength Spanx could hold up the mass, and I could hide martini olives under the bags beneath my eyes. I concluded that something drastic had to be done immediately if I was ever going to bed with something other than my Pearl Rabbit vibrator.

I began to research medical professionals in the area who could transform me back into the hot chick I was twenty-five years ago. Yes, I still believe in miracles. I went to my first appointment with a positive attitude and a credit card. Both were necessary.

For the first procedure, I had my uvula cut off. Right there in the doctor's office. My uvula was swollen and painful, so the doctor said it had to be removed. He threw it away, but I don't miss it.

Please note that a uvula is different from a *vulva*. The uvula is the appendage that hangs down from the back of your throat and contributes to snoring. *That's* what got the guillotine. A vulva is the external genital organ of a female. I'm keeping that part.

So anyway, at the doctor's office, he numbed my mouth, stabbed the uvula with a long, threaded needle, sliced off the offending body part, and pulled it out with the thread. I asked him why he didn't keep all of the butchered uvulas and string them around his office. He didn't think I was funny. Maybe that's because he doesn't have a vulva. I think I'm funnier than any plastic surgeon. The procedure seemed to work because I no longer wake myself with ravaged nasal sounds that resemble a passing freight train.

Then I signed up for a free consultation from one of Idaho's leading plastic surgeons. I was embarrassed about my body because I had willingly given birth to monster babies: my first child weighed almost ten pounds at birth, and the second was eleven pounds. I didn't have any more children after that. During pregnancy, my fifty-inch belly was so big that buttons popped off my maternity blouses. Never one to miss dinner, I had to wedge my dinner plate on top of my belly and beneath my gigantic boobs that had morphed into two bulging bags of the baby's instant meals.

My legs remained normal, so I looked like a gigantic blob wobbling about on two spindles. I couldn't turn sideways while going through a doorway, and I forgot what my feet looked like. It was a minor miracle that I could sit down without popping. By the ninth month, getting out of a chair required a hoist and a greased pulley system. Strangers would touch my belly with the same shock and fascination used to examine a beached whale. I remember some of the more interesting comments:

"Looky here, Wendy. Aren't you glad you never got THAT big?"

"Good Lord! You got triplets in there? You're the biggest woman I've ever seen!"

"Your belly's going to drag on the floor after that one comes out! My cousin was huge like you, and she never walked right again. Then her husband left her. She died soon after."

I made mental notes to include these people as sinister characters in future short stories. It would be great fun to write about their untimely catastrophes and mysterious bouts of ghastly, tongue-eating diseases.

As a result of my pregnancies, I had two marvelous children but a damaged body. My waist refused to go back where it came from, and, after two years of nursing, my breasts were like swaying punching bags. In a strong wind, I was in danger of toppling over, never to get upright again. I could store books and snacks in my cleavage, and I haven't worn a button-up blouse in thirty years. My bra was a size 42 Long.

Anyway, I went to get my free consultation about how to tighten up my sagging belly and maybe raise my breasts up off the floor. At the doctor's office, I was greeted by a gorgeous young woman with a perfect body. I knew instantly that she was a walking billboard for the plastic surgeon, mainly because she looked plastic. Her face was so tight she couldn't change her expression even if she sat her skinny butt on burning coals.

And her flat stomach would show a bump if she swallowed an olive. My granddaughters have paper dolls that are thicker. I immediately hated her—and she looked at me and returned the same opinion. She told me to put on a pair of teeny panties that were sized for a stripper and wait for the doctor. I don't usually undress for strangers unless plied with expensive liquor, but I did as I was told.

The doctor entered with a dashing flair of haughty perfection; he had a chiseled jaw, tight skin, and not an ounce of body fat. He looked at me and caught his breath. I was the perfect candidate for his advertisements that revealed the "before" photograph…the one that shows just how grotesque the human body can become. And his imagined "after" photo would reveal his amazing skills that could save all of humanity from the offensive sight of me!

As if to magnify my humiliation, he turned on a spotlight and brought out a Sharpie pen. Then with the flair of a great artist he drew circles all over my matronly body, humming to himself with each new design until my body looked like the distorted hide of a spotted giraffe. Then he added arrows—as if plotting a map of hidden treasure buried somewhere within the undulating folds of fat. During this time, I was imagining how many ways I could kill myself.

He finished his artwork and then took photos, assuring me that my face wouldn't be in the photographs. At that point, my face was by far cuter than my body. Then he told me to turn around so he could get shots of my backside. I assumed he had a wide-angle lens. By then, I was making mental notes about how to destroy the office and the doctor…and how to take out his obnoxious mannequin assistant. I drooled at the thought of watching her bony body blow up into a clattering pile of kindling. (Okay, some therapy might have been needed at this point.)

The doctor left the torture room, so I dressed quickly and was ushered into his elaborate office. It reeked of excess, and so did my body. I felt like shit.

The doctor explained the various procedures I needed and offered a special deal if I had more than one. That special deal cost enough money to buy a car. I sat up straight, sucked in my offensive belly, and marched my imperfect, Sharpie-stained body out of his office. And I cancelled any further appointments. Then I left to daydream at the car lot.

I wasn't ready to give up, so I decided to start with a smaller area, noting that my eyes were less fat than my thighs. I compiled recommendations from tight-eyed friends, reviewed several doctors, and scheduled a consultation with a delightful female surgeon. It was easier to accept the cost when we agreed that the procedure would improve my vision. I eagerly scheduled an appointment for her to render me unconscious, cut underneath my eyes, and lift my eyelids. What could go wrong?

"This is the most fat I've ever removed!" the perky doctor greeted me as I woke from the drug-induced slumber. I tried to focus as she held out a surgical napkin holding two plump lines of slime that resembled skinned worms.

"Look at this!" She seemed breathless. "All this came from under your eyes!"

I was still on a happy high from the drugs. "Can you imagine what you'd get if you sucked out my belly!" I said. "You'd need to bring in a wheelbarrow and a shovel!"

She was giddy about her prize and turned to show the other doctors, who proceeded to gasp and look over at me. Yes, that's the day I became known as the Obese Eye Lady— the one who produced the most eyeball fat ever removed in the history of a medical procedure known as blepharoplasty. I waved and went back to sleep, wondering how in the hell I could get more of the delightful drugs.

The next day, I woke to find a raccoon staring back at me in the mirror. The hideous bruises under my eyes were black and looked as if I had been the loser in a brawl at the women's prison. For the next four weeks, those bruises migrated slowly down my cheeks, turning green and then yellow, until they landed on my chin, which by then was sprouting a scraggly beard.

After about a month, the bruises went away—just about the time that the bags returned, as if to mock the thousands of dollars I had spent on the procedure.

I finally resorted to two proven methods that could help boost my sagging body and spirit. Consume less and exercise more. Not a totally original concept, and the only knife involved would be used to cut up vegetables. To help fix my figure of flab, I enrolled in a physical fitness program taught by my drill sergeant daughter. I did my best to keep up with healthy women half my age, and the program helped reduce flabby arms and tighten my sponge-like belly. I threw away the bags of M&M candies and the oversized black tunics, and I cut down on wine consumption. *Cut down*. Not abstained. I regularly sipped wine, for medicinal purposes only. Finally I lost enough weight to wear white pants again in public.

My claim to fame in the exercise program I'm enrolled in is that I can do a body plank for seven minutes, and the Spandex-clad youngsters can't. Holding a plank that long causes every part of my body to be tight, except my cheeks. They still jiggle.

~

Midlife Dating and Mating

Nothing screams "pathetic loser" like being a middle-aged divorcee alone at a festive party where beautiful couples are trading sloppy kisses and giggling like demented clowns. There's not enough spiked punch in the world to soften the pain of pretending it doesn't matter. Many of us graze along the buffet table hoping the crunch of nachos will be louder than the boisterous laughter of young lovers, and then we migrate to the bar because all we get to take home is a headache.

We never intended to be divorced at midlife because we were programmed to believe the happily-ever-after deceptions that provided easy and convenient endings in fairy tales. But according to a recent study by Bowling Green State University in Ohio, the divorce rate among people age forty-six to sixty-four has grown more than 50 percent. Almost one-third of baby boomers are single, either by divorce, separation, or having never been married. Some are attracted to the single lifestyle while others would trade their original Beatles record collection for some hot passion.

Those of you past the age of forty-five know that growing older can be a cruel trick of nature. You used to be able to drop five pounds overnight and wear a swimsuit sized for a toddler. Now you look at a cookie and instantly gain ten pounds. I exercise regularly just to maintain this above-average weight. If I didn't work out, I'd need to move into a box car with sliding doors.

I have several friends who have been married to their husbands for more than thirty years. They're happy and comfortable and couldn't imagine dating at this stage of life. And if something drastic happened to their husbands, at their ages they would rather join a cloistered convent than get naked in front of another man. They wouldn't want to have to worry about unpredictable, middle-aged dilemmas such as the sudden crazy mood swings and chronic irritable bowel syndrome that could make for an awkward first date.

I faced a Christmas alone while in my fifties. I unpacked the decorations and forced myself to set up a tree, but the ornaments reminded me of a past life, one that was broken beyond repair. So I turned to retail therapy and bought new ornaments, but it wasn't the same. Deck the halls with strange boughs of holly was a different song, and I didn't know the verses.

I survived until the wonderful day of December 26 when the world returned to normal. Hairdressers, mailmen, and waiters didn't need to perk up for an extra tip, egg nog wasn't tempting me at the grocery store, and children didn't care if the silly elf on the shelf was watching because they had eleven free months to misbehave. And divorced people could return to work and focus on important things, such as how to lose the extra ten pounds gained while gobbling an entire pecan pie alone on Christmas Eve.

When I was single, my friends just assumed I would be coming solo to any future functions. I'd be the single woman they would pair with the disgruntled, crazy uncle at dinner parties or the one they called to babysit on Valentine's Day because I didn't have anything else to do. Well, I was determined to prove them wrong.

Soon after my winter of discontent, some friends invited me to dinner. They just happened to have a recently divorced guest who was visiting from another state. I never turn down a free meal, so I agreed to join them. I met him and instantly felt a connection. He was in his fifties and ruggedly handsome. At dinner, our knees touched under the table during the salad course. We laughed at silly jokes during the entrée, and by dessert, he was feeding me bites of cheesecake. I felt like a goofy teenager.

This marvelous man met all my requirements: He was middle-aged, single, and didn't wear white socks with sandals. (At my age, you can't get too picky.) As an added bonus, though, he was handsome, smart, employed, passionate, and he wanted to know about my children. It was like winning the Publishers Clearing House Sweepstakes, the lottery, and top-shelf wine at happy hour all at the same time.

We spent four days together, often to the chagrin of his abandoned hosts, and then I took him to the airport. It was a scene out of *Casablanca*, complete with winter fog and drama. He held me close and whispered, "We'll always have Boise." Then he tipped his hat, sauntered through security, and hollered, "Here's looking at you, Kid."

I drove home, wondering if he remembered my real name wasn't Kid. But it didn't matter. I was smitten, and it felt good. To paraphrase a quote from the movie, of all the towns in all the world, he walked into mine. He called when he landed at the next airport and was about to change planes. "I think this is the beginning of a beautiful relationship," he said.

"Say it again," I said, "for old times' sake."

And, yes, at that moment we were Humphrey Bogart and Ingrid Bergman but without the messy Nazi and farewell-forever scenes.

We enjoyed a long-distance relationship over the next few months. When you talk on the telephone, you really get to know someone without the physical distractions. After two months of fabulous phone fantasy, he made plans to return to Idaho. We embraced in the airport like long-lost lovers. I'm pretty sure a crew from central casting yelled "Action!" as we clung together in frantic passion. I'm positive I even heard music from a mysterious gospel choir.

At midlife, adults know what they want and don't want. There is no time for games because we never know when we'll get struck by a bus or wander onto a bus and end up in Kansas without our little dog Toto. We accept our partner's wrinkles and well-earned laugh lines, and we're positively giddy that we can enjoy romance again. My more-than-significant other got a job in Idaho, moved in with me, and we never looked back. He loves my children, and I love his. One benefit of middle-aged relationships is that there aren't any potential in-law issues to handle. Our one surviving parent has dementia and can't remember our names.

Once comfortable in our relationship, I nicknamed him Studley, for obvious reasons. The fact that he took a chance on me is nothing short of a minor miracle. Here are just a few of the circumstances that we endured while dating:

The Age Conundrum. I'm five years older, but I didn't want him to know that. We visited my mountain cabin, and I rushed in first to remove a framed poem I had on the wall. The poem was my first national publication, and it listed the year it was published and included the fact that I was only twelve years old. I didn't want him to see the inscription, compute my age, and then look at his watch and say, "Well, it's time to go."

Bare Boobs at the Birthday Bash. It's always interesting the first time you introduce your boyfriend to your family. Studley lived 1,700 miles away, so we had a long-distance relationship for nine months. One time he flew to Idaho when my daughter was having a birthday party for her two-year-old daughter. We arrived just in time for him to meet both my children, their spouses, their children, my mother, and my ex-husband and his girlfriend. Also, there were several women openly breastfeeding their babies. Poor Studley didn't know where to look, so he spent the afternoon talking with my elderly mother. She still doesn't remember who he is.

An Affair to Forget. Probably the stupidest thing we did while dating happened when my mother was staying at my house. Studley flew in from Texas, and we wanted to be together, but out of respect for my mother, we decided he should stay overnight at the neighbor's house. Well, he didn't leave at midnight as planned, so at dawn, when it was 32 degrees out, he tiptoed out the back door and snuck over to the neighbor's house, which was much farther away than he had remembered. Freezing cold—he was still wearing the shorts and sandals he had arrived in—he tried all their doors, but they were locked. He finally managed to get in through the garage. And, yes, we were both in our fifties and acting like guilty people having affairs. I still apologize for that one. Besides, with Mom's dementia she probably assumed we were some nice couple who had been married several decades.

The Late Limousine. One time he was scheduled to fly to see me, and I was giddy about how to meet him at the airport. I scheduled a limousine and had the backseat stocked with Johnny Walker Blue Label Scotch and an order of chicken wings from Hooters. Nothing says romance like expensive scotch and chicken wings from a big-breasted diva! Then I wore a tight dress, push-up bra, and sultry expression.

But the limousine was late, and his plane had landed by the time we arrived at the airport. I jumped out and went running up the escalator. "Hey, Ambrose!" he hollered, going down the escalator next to mine. I had to finish going all the way up the escalator and then come back down. My sultry attitude got lost along the way.

The limousine couldn't wait at the curb, so it circled the airport while we shivered outside. By the time the limo finally arrived, the chicken wings were cold—but it didn't matter. We had those windows steamed up by the time the limo hit the freeway.

Proof that I'm no Porn Star. After several months, our fun relationship developed into a torrid love affair. He called me every morning to wake me up, and I pretended to be alert and cheerful, even though I'm not a morning person. We made plans for our next rendezvous, so I wanted to give him a special surprise—even better than a limousine stocked with scotch and chicken wings.

I'm not that experienced at being sexy. After all, I grew up on an isolated potato and pig farm in southern Idaho, and I preferred reading and writing over being risqué. Now, well into a midlife relationship, I wanted to go to the next level but wasn't sure how to get out of first gear. So I donned a disguise with a raincoat, hat, and dark glasses and visited a local "pleasure" store. I gasped when I saw the displays. Who needs a three-foot, glowing, purple dildo? Maybe I don't want to know. And what's the point of wearing crotchless panties? Just take off everything.

Anyway, the sales lady assured me that the strawberry-flavored gel was guaranteed to drive a man wild. I bought a tube and hid it in the nightstand. The first night he arrived, I told him I had a special treat. I lit candles, turned down the lights, and asked him to lie face-down and naked on the bed for a sensual massage.

In the darkness, I couldn't read the instructions on the tube, and I was too vain to put on my glasses. So I started to apply what I thought was massage oil onto his back, his legs, and his arms. The substance was more like marmalade. Then I tried brushing his skin with a long feather—but it got stuck in the goo. There were no warnings on the package to predict such a disaster. Suddenly he looked like a feathered jam sandwich. Neither of us was aroused by the experience. After he got up to take a hot shower to degrease, I got my glasses and read that the magical gel was intended for one specific body part—and that wasn't on his back. I haven't had strawberry jam since. And I'm returning the French maid costume. And the riding whip and handcuffs.

Not Fit for the Blood Drive. Because we only got together once or twice a month, it was an action-packed experience every time we met. After one particularly steamy visit, he returned to Texas to donate blood for the community blood drive. After they took a sample, he was declined, and it wasn't because of illegal drugs or a recent tattoo. He didn't have enough iron to qualify to donate blood. Let's just say he spent a lot of energy in Idaho.

We married on an island in Greece with a bevy of Greeks who couldn't speak English. We sang, ate, and danced beside the sea. The following Christmas, we hung mistletoe over the doorway, and in front of children and grandchildren, we kissed, much longer than necessary. We celebrated our current love and future journey, ever mindful that we could have missed this splendid opportunity for happiness. Occasionally I'll bring home a cheesecake to refresh the memories of our first dinner together. We share a few bites, floss and take our vitamins, and then turn down the lights.

Marriage at midlife doesn't guarantee total bliss, but we've discovered that laughter is better than breaking something or shooting someone. Every morning I get online and read reports of treachery, debauchery, and ghastly evilness. And that's just from the local garden club. There is so much grief, angst, quarreling, and pure nastiness in our country that some of my over-fifty friends want to hide in the cellar with a barrel of nuts, a few gallons of wine, a year's supply of chocolate, and a battery-operated device to help ease their frustrations.

Don't allow that to happen. Surround yourself with funny people, avoid the bitter, crabby ones, and laugh until an adult beverage runs out of your nose. Take another chance on love; either rekindle a long-time marriage or, if you're single, find a companion who's eager to share all the fun and frustrations of life.

I want to grow old sitting on the patio with Studley. He'll be sipping a smooth Scotch—with or without chicken wings—and I'll have a nice cabernet...or two...or three. And like fine wine, life will just get better with age.

Based upon my experience of finding sweet love after a sour midlife divorce, I have a few tips for how to cope with being single until that happens.

1. Having a sense of humor and a sassy attitude is essential if you want to survive. A divorced woman often feels like a lone loser in a world full of happy, laughing couples. When I was invited to a New Year's Eve party several years ago, I did what any forty-five-year-old divorced woman would do. I rented a costume complete with velvet gown, a jeweled crown, and ornate scepter and went as "The Queen of Everything." There was that awkward moment at midnight when couples were kissing and I dug into the artichoke dip with a vengeance, but otherwise it was a grand celebration of independence and a fresh beginning.

2. Channel your inner drill sergeant. My priorities then were to take care of my children and myself. Dating was not important, mainly because I was too busy learning how to climb two ladders: one to clean out the rain gutters and the other to advance my career as I managed household finances, completed my job as editor at a local magazine, and monitored my son's teenage parties in the basement.

3. Stop being a victim and learn to laugh again. To put it bluntly: divorce sucks. I'm not proud to have joined the 50 percent of US married couples that are divorced, but I'm sassier because of it, and my children are employed members of society and happily married with children. With personal trauma and drama, I turn to humor to keep me from causing great harm to people or objects. Some people use inspirational quotes to sustain them; I use comedy.

"Marriage is probably the chief cause of divorce," according to Larry Gelbart, the wonderful comedy writer who developed the hit television show *M*A*S*H*.

Another astute comedienne, Rita Rudner, often says, "Whenever I date a guy, I think, *Is this the man I want my children to spend their weekends with?*"

And one more quip for the middle-age crowd: these days, parents pray the youngest child will get married and move out before the oldest one gets divorced and moves back in.

Humor helps me from morphing into Sissy Spacek's character in *Carrie*. What woman wouldn't love to have telekinetic powers for just one day to seek revenge on all those who have done her wrong? Especially at the prom! But I wouldn't look good in prison orange, so I reduce the angst by writing, reading funny books, and consuming copious quantities of red wine.

4. Don't divorce the entire gang. One major negative of divorce is how quickly a person comes into and goes out of a family. I miss my ex-sisters-in-law; it's too bad the in-law package is lawfully attached to the marriage. We communicate through social media, and I appreciate

the ability to keep in touch. I don't like the "ex" label for everyone, so I hereby officially declare that we are still sisters. I respect my ex-father-in-law and send him a card on special occasions. My children remain cousins with nieces and nephews of my ex-husband, and I encourage their friendships. Reducing drama takes skill and talent, plus the ability to regularly discern the difference between a cheap zinfandel from a robust cabernet.

And here are some tips for finding love after divorce at midlife:

- **Don't look for it.** I had no intention of falling in love with my dinner partner. I just wanted a good meal but ended up with extra dessert.

- **Stay healthy and exercise regularly.** You don't want a middle-aged partner who's a lazy, smelly slob, so don't be one either.

- **Keep busy.** Find activities you enjoy and groups that appreciate your talents. Hang out with positive people and avoid crabby people at pity parties.

- **Avoid the temptation to settle.** Make a list of your non-negotiable requirements in a partner. Include politics, religion, money management, in-laws, and if they sleep with their pets. The less critical issues, such as chores and hobbies, can be mitigated if your prospective lover has a delightful sense of humor. (If many of us had made the list the first time, maybe the divorces could have been avoided.)

- **Wear sexy panties every day.** No one else will see them, but you'll feel like a woman who's comfortable in her own skin and refuses to be frumpy. Even though I'm a proud grandma, I still love silky, lacy underwear.

- **Believe in yourself.** Maybe you won't find true love for years, but remember that a long marriage doesn't necessarily mean success. Watch older couples together, and you'll see many who don't communicate and others who look bitter. Choose to emulate the couples who still hold hands, make regular eye contact, and enjoy public displays of affection. Assume they're married to each other. Finally, as you should know by now, it's okay to be independent all by yourself.

If you're divorced, you realize something went wrong with your failed marriage. You can learn from the painful experience, get up again, adjust your crown, and take another chance on finding love. It could be waiting right there between the entrée and the cheesecake.

$\sim$

Arousing Fifty Shades of Grey Matter

The owner of a hotel in England recently replaced guest copies of the Holy Bible, the world's bestselling book, with *Fifty Shades of Grey,* the soft-porn bestseller than inspires horny women to imagine torrid but poorly written fantasies. While I endorse creative marketing strategies and applaud freedom of physical expression, I can only assume that the hotel management will also provide locked safes for families with children, and disposable, battery-operated toys for those flying solo.

Because I can't stop myself from noticing the profound and conspicuous differences between the two books, I've noted an excerpt from each:

> *"As the apple tree among the trees of the wood, so is my beloved among men. I sat down under his shadow with great delight, and his fruit was sweet to my taste....*
> *Let him kiss me with the kisses of his mouth,*
> *for (his) love is more delightful than wine."*

—"Song of Solomon," Old Testament, written 3,000 years ago

"I found some baby oil. Let me rub it on your behind."

—*Fifty Shades of Grey,* current bestselling novel

I don't want to debate religion (thank God). I'm merely questioning the literary value of certain bestselling books. It doesn't take much imagination to slither into Anastasia Steele's sticky bedroom where she exclaims with amazement, "I don't remember reading about nipple clamps in the Bible!" But it takes thought and reflection to get lost in *Bel Canto* by Ann Patchett (a personal favorite) or to feel the heartache described in *The Help* by Kathryn Stockett or to appreciate the wit of Olive Ann Burns in *Cold Sassy Tree.* Maybe it's all a matter of balancing excellence with trash, much like enjoying the occasional corn dog at the fair. But it's also important to use or lose the delicate sensory perception abilities that come from our brains to arouse the gray matter between our ears instead of between the sheets.

Ironically, there is a subtle connection with *Fifty Shades of Grey* and *A Tale of Two Cities,* the all-time bestselling novel ever written. Biographers of the author Charles Dickens wrote that he believed that prolific sexual activity was necessary for a healthy man. The sub-plot for his great novel centers on the sexual exploitation of a young, powerless girl by an older, powerful man. Sounds like the prelude to *Fifty Shades.*

A real lover doesn't just show affection on Valentine's Day, also commonly known as Guilt Your Partner into Giving You Roses and Chocolates Day. Many middle-aged couples aren't fooled by the February hype that equates true love with big diamonds. Some are actually smug in their firm belief that a kiss every day outlasts lingerie.

The National Retail Federation predicts that $18.6 billion will be spent this year on Valentine's Day gifts that include jewelry, flowers, candy, and greeting cards. Most couples over the age of fifty ignore the hype and prefer a nice dinner with fine wine, a slow dance on the patio, and a tender look that says, "I will love you forever. Have you seen my reading glasses?"

The Valentine's Day edition of a popular women's magazine offered some provocative advice about how to drive a man crazy by using naughty costumes that take a backstage crew to lace up and high-heeled shoes that are sharp and long enough to stack a dozen donuts. At midlife, most of us would rather strut out wearing an easy-off costume with Velcro sides, dim the lights, turn on some Luther Vandross, and holler, "Come and get it!" before it's time for the evening news and a dose of iron pills.

The passing years have provided us the wisdom to know that if we donned a skimpy outfit smaller than a hanky and then wore a blindfold, we would trip over our wobbly stilettos and smack our head on the nightstand. And if we lit fifty candles and then agreed to handcuffs, we'd knock over the candles, set the house on fire, and not be able to find the key to the cuffs. Our friendly firemen would be greatly amused and Tweet our hapless images to the world.

Most women at midlife are strong advocates for romance, but we want and need it more than once a year. We prefer daily acts of devotion that can build a lasting love affair. My sweetheart makes my coffee every morning and brings me the newspaper. (Yes, a morning newspaper proves just how old we are.) He laughs at my jokes even though he's heard them before and they're really not that funny. And he kisses me every night and morning. We touch in our sleep, and that is the essence of pure love.

True romance often requires a sense of humor. I don't mind trying new amorous adventures, but they often come with comical and unromantic results. The kitchen table was way too hard, the secluded outside picnic came with ants and thorns, and the tight corset took thirty minutes to remove. And after a romantic dinner and a bottle of fine wine, it's not wise to spend more than ten minutes getting glamorous for bed. He'll already be asleep.

Single, middle-aged women shouldn't give up on passion; it's just too much fun. Millions of people over fifty enjoy loving relationships, and they now comprise the biggest group in online dating. According to the Mayo Foundation for Medical Education and Research, sexual health is important at any age, and doctors agree that older couples that enjoy sexual intimacy can lower their blood pressure, reduce the risks of heart attacks, and look years younger. A festive romp in the hay is a grand way to end the day, and there is no medical study required for that astute observation.

As millions of American women grow closer to age sixty, we no longer relate to the role models of yesterday. We reject the weathered images of sixty-three-year-old Irene Ryan as Granny Clampett in the television series *Beverly Hillbillies* and prefer the strong image of sixty-three-year-old movie star Meryl Streep. We love the feisty spirits of sexy senior citizens Betty White and Tina Turner. Television legend Joan Collins is seventy-nine years young. At a pre-Grammy party in Beverly Hills, she said that sex was better than Botox for slowing the aging process. In response, many of

Mother Bear

I used to feed my little ones with a spoon shaped like an airplane. Now they open their mouths every time they hear a plane. But we had great fun during mealtime. I'd strap their wiggly body into the highchair and begin the mommy dance of getting most of the food into their body. The airplane spoon worked best, and we had great travel adventures right there in the kitchen.

"Here it comes, (airplane noises), open up for a magical delivery from Ireland!"

The animation worked until I tried to sneak in blended peas or stewed prunes. Then even the most daring and high-diving airplane spoon couldn't open the steel mouth of refusal. (Really, can you blame them?) But this pilot was no dummy. Sprinkle a few berries on top of the concoction, and that fortress opened faster than the mouse ran up the clock.

What's up with wee toddlers sucking food out of pouches? Now clever marketers and busy parents have discovered food pouches that offer quick, easy, and convenient ways to feed babies. Slap on an "organic" label, and you can dash out the door guilt-free. Just don't forget to take the baby.

Experts with long titles now question the overuse of food pouches. They point to complications with tooth decay, proper oral development, and socialization issues. I don't need a professional title to see the biggest problem. A special experience is lost when a toddler is strapped into a back car seat sucking food from a bag while Mommy is swearing as she maneuvers through traffic. I say bring back the airplane spoon, sit down face to face, and have some fun. Delightful toddlers have a way of turning into aloof teenagers, so enjoy a captive audience while you can.

Because I'm older, experienced, and cheerfully sarcastic, I chuckle at all the "new" advancements for young parents. Cloth diapers. Homemade baby food. Organized playdates. Baby monitors with live-streaming videos. DVDs that instruct clueless parents how to introduce their children to music, nature, and art. And it's truly a miracle that previous generations of portable babies ever survived without a stroller that was bigger than a Volkswagen.

In my day, disposable diapers were too expensive, so the only choice was the one-size-fits-all cloth. And pinning them on a wiggly baby often resulted in accidental stabbings, but only to my clumsy thumbs. I developed the skills of an intricate, highly-skilled technician as I made goo-goo faces to distract the little cherub and secured the bulky diaper. Soiled diapers were dunked in the toilet and stored in a hamper until washed and reused. There was no alternative other than to allow the brood to run around naked in a pen that could be washed with a high-pressure hose. That option did cross my mind a few times.

Now with disposables, it's just strap on a synthetic polymer and fibrous pad made from wood pulp and absorbent chemicals and toss the used ones in the garbage. The average baby goes through 8,000 diapers, and about 20 billion are dumped into landfills each year. They don't degrade well and take about 500 years to decompose. At least old cloth diapers can be reused to wash the car and dust the patio furniture.

I would like to take this self-righteous opportunity to remind my children to thank me because I never made them wear chemically-treated wood chips on their precious little butts. However, given the choice between dunking poop-filled diapers and tossing the offending package into the garbage, I would have appreciated the second option. Every time.

Now, let's discuss the new and exciting innovation of homemade baby food. Did you know that parents can take regular food and smash it into mush to make it easier to feed their babies? I suspect this technique was used by all the generations that survived before 1927 when Mrs. Dan Gerber, the wife of a Michigan canning company owner, asked her husband for help in straining peas for their infant daughter. Now Gerber sells 190 products in eighty countries. In 2007, Gerber was sold to Nestlé for $5.5 billion. Well played, Mrs. Gerber.

I tried to use processed baby food. In fact, I cut out a picture of the Gerber baby from a cereal box and taped it to the underside of the kitchen cabinet. Then I placed my baby boy in a carrier and set it on the counter so he could stare at the picture as I fed him. He loved it. I still have that picture, and no one gets it until after I die.

Anyway, baby food wasn't enough for him. That could be because he weighed twenty pounds at four months and soon was too big to fit into the carrier. I couldn't lift him onto the counter anymore, so I tied him into his big sister's highchair. He preferred soup, mashed potatoes, and hamburger. By age one, he was gnawing on steak bones. If I had offered him a pouch of processed baby food, he would have toddled out the door and attacked the neighbor's cat. No, we didn't use much baby food at our house.

There was no need to organize play dates when my kids were young. We lived in a neighborhood with young families, and there was usually a gaggle of giggling girls in one home or the other. The little boys would be stomping in mud puddles and falling off fences. One neighbor and I traded babysitting twice a week. It was the only free time we had to run errands, go to appointments, read a book, or go to the bathroom in peace and quiet. One day, my eighteen-month-old son was irritated because all the girls were playing in the neighbor's bedroom and they shut the door. So, he broke down the door. I still feel bad about that.

I don't intend to sound sexist, but it's true that little girls and boys play differently. When the girls came to our house, they danced, sang silly songs, and played dress-up while the boys were in the yard seeing who could poop in the grass like a dog. My son was proud to be the usual winner. He got over that a few years ago.

He's now a father of a fabulous little girl, and I'm often lucky enough to watch her. It's amusing to bite my tongue and nod politely as he lectures me about the procedures: "Here are the diapers, here is the feeding schedule, here is a ten-page list of emergency contacts, and here is the baby monitor." I noticed the video showed her quietly sleeping in her crib, but I already knew this without needing a live-streaming picture. They tiptoed out the door, reminding me to hold up the baby's head when I lifted her. I hand-palmed my forehead and gushed with gratitude for the wise instructions. Who knew?

The $50 billion baby care products industry includes lotions, potions, and diapers. A baby needs a few of these items. Less crucial is the emerging multi-million-dollar market for DVDs that claim to transform your silly little kid into a genius who's better than the other kids. I'm not fond of children spouting scientific data when they still need a nightlight and a potty chair.

The baby genius market promises to "engage babies and provide parents with tools to help expose their little ones to the world around them by stimulating the baby's natural curiosity." Right. Perch a toddler in front of a screen, grab a beer, and wait for the enlightenment. Or, here's a better idea. Try taking them outside to sit on a blanket to watch the leaves flutter as the clouds make funny formations. Introduce music by playing various rhythms and sharing childproof instruments. Instill a love of arts through picture books, paints, and play dough. And show them nature by taking them to the zoo, or planning a day trip to the mountains, or pretending to have adventures in the back-yard. No DVD player is required. If you do this often, then you can justify an all-day Disney marathon while you kick back in sweats with a platter of cookies.

A recent study discovered that babies who watch videos have less cognitive understanding of words than infants who do not watch them. Other studies indicate that daily reading and storytelling are associated with increases in language skills. I loved to tell stories to my children, and now I get to perform Storytelling Part 3,286 to my grand-kids. Yes, I can conjure up fabulous tales of magical uni-corns and secret meadows and wonderful adventures—and I don't even need inspiration from wine. Not until their par-ents take them home. Then I have a bottle uncorked before their car leaves my driveway.

Once I had my grandkids overnight, and their parents left a contraption that was innocently labeled a stroller but required a NASA instruction manual. I've seen television sets with fewer components. It was a double-seater, mean-ing twice the frustration. While the darling children were taking a nap, I refused the temptation to join them and tried to open the stroller. After considerable effort in maneu-vering levers and manipulating various mechanisms, the buggy sprang into a hulking machine that filled my entire living room. I was chagrined when I realized I would need to collapse the damn thing to get it out the door.

I never had a stroller, but that worked to my advantage. I toted my off-the-growth-chart children everywhere, and as a result I developed the arms of a professional wrestler. That's probably why I can hold a body plank for seven min-utes. And with a simple flex, I can cause door-to-door sales-people to drop their pamphlets, apologize, and run away. Once the bundles of joy passed fifty pounds I told them it was time to walk on their own, so they picked up their backpacks and went to school. In spite of their mother, my children grew up to become successful adults.

I'm not picking on young parents. Well, maybe I am, and if so, I apologize. But I have the perspective of look-ing back to observe what worked and what didn't. I worked outside the home before having children and then stayed home with them for five years while my husband worked, and then I returned to full-time employment. It's a luxury to stay home, but we lived on a small amount of money in a small house. There weren't any unnecessary expenses, and yet we survived just fine. I treasure those years when my two little children and I played house together.

When my kids were teenagers, we had a large basement, and I enjoyed inviting their friends over for pizza parties. The peace of mind was worth the clutter, noise, expense, and assorted chaos. Years later, I often encounter some of those teens who are now productive young adults. They fondly recount stories about those years, and not one of them served time in jail or became a television evangelist. I'm happy about that.

Now my son works in law enforcement, and his job often requires him to enter homes where good parenting skills aren't a priority. It's difficult to prepare a nutritious family meal when the kitchen has been converted into a meth lab and the naked toddler is drinking from the dog's bowl.

Fortunately for me, because of these horrible conditions, my son now believes that I was Mother of the Year and that it wasn't so bad when I served macaroni and leftover meat-loaf for dinner six nights out of seven during his formative years. At least I occasionally added raisins or a can of olives as a creative side dish. He also understands why I was known as the Mother Bear of Centennial High School.

Yes, I was one of those mothers—the one who wanted to know her children's friends, where they were going, and what time they would be home. My daughter still hasn't forgiven me for panicking when she missed a high school curfew. I started calling everyone, including her school principal. She'll understand in ten years when she has a teenager.

I was stunned when my daughter became the age I was when she was born. How could that be? Wasn't it only yesterday that I sewed her a little dress to match my homemade blouse? Didn't I just tote her in a backpack to explore the great outdoors—and then dig a live wasp out of her mouth? I still remember the piano recitals, the dance recitals, and the stage performances. I was the obnoxious mother in the front row with the camera. (Now she's toting her own little girls…along with the camera and hopes and dreams.)

To celebrate her birthday, I took her to *Menopause the Musical.* It's hilarious, and we laughed together. The musical reminded her to enjoy life now before middle age brings the challenges of incontinence, sagging skin, weight gain, memory lapse, and mood swings. After our evening, I was so happy I rushed home to sew us matching outfits. I hope she'll be pleasantly surprised.

In my humble opinion, there are three ways to raise amazing children: First, love them—fiercely, totally, and unconditionally. Second, set an example by your words and actions. Don't expect them to get academic scholarships if you haven't read a book in twenty years. Third, get lucky. We all know good parents who have bad children, and vice versa.

Now that my adult children have children of their own, I'm amazed at how well they are doing as parents. There is tremendous stress on young families today, and I admit they deserve the conveniences of strollers, movies, and prepared baby food. And now that I babysit the grandkids, I'll vouch for the necessity of disposable diapers. My childhood was full of freedom—we played outside until dark, never wore a helmet, and our only telephone was attached to a wall back home. I worry about my grandchildren in our brave new world, but I know they're in good hands and come from a strong foundation. And they don't live too far from this devoted Grandmother Bear.

At this stage of life, I have a new appreciation for raising children. Recently I waited behind a young woman in line at the grocery store. Her three kids were simultaneously crying, kicking each other, opening cereal boxes, and sneezing until green goo dripped down their chins. I made eye contact with the frazzled mother and gave her the "this too shall pass" smile. She meekly smiled back and then wrestled her wild, snotty brood out the door. Suddenly I adored the age spots on my hands.

Most of us have been there. We take our darling little angels into public places, but suddenly and inexplicably they become possessed by behavior demons that turn them into outrageous monsters. We begin the polite, hushed cajoling, which fails miserably, so we resort to bribery. "Yes, honey pie, just be patient and then you can have an ice-cream cone. Not enough? How about a pony?"

Some adults skip the bartering and go straight for the barking. Recently I witnessed a frightening display of questionable parenting at a big discount store. A loud woman wearing flannel pajama pants and a Hawaiian shirt yelled at her two wild and disheveled children, "Stop punchin' the bread or I'll kick your ass!" Then she threw a six-pack of beer onto the bread and barreled down the aisle as her spirited spawn wrestled on the floor. I predict incarceration in the future. For all of them.

A generation ago, bad behavior resulted in a firm swat across the butt. While momentarily effective, physical punishment doesn't address the reason for the public temper tantrum. And although quite tempting, it's not a good idea to just leave your kids in the store's Kiddy Corral and drive home with a gallon of ice cream.

For an interesting perspective, harried mothers and sneering critics should trade places with raucous children. Imagine you're stuffed into a grocery cart piled high with food as your tired parent pushes you through tall corridors of colorful packages. You're lost in the commotion, and you don't have a clue about money, jobs, house payments, or that Mommy only gets four hours of sleep every night. You just know it would be great fun to open the peanut butter and smear it in Sister's hair and make her scream. Now *that* would get Mommy's attention.

Here's some unsolicited advice for stressed young mothers:

1. Children are noisy, messy, curious, hungry, tired, dirty, funny, adorable, little people who are here because of Mommy and Daddy. Yes, they're your fault and your responsibility.

2. Remember that your toddler has only two years of experience in being alive, and you have only that much experience in being her/his mother. So, you can't expect perfection after only two years of on-the-job training. And you're surrounded by countless other parents and toddlers who are trying to figure out the directions.

3. Sometimes parenthood sucks. Once I dumped a glass of milk on my child's head because he was throwing a fit

and I didn't know what else to do. We were both shocked, and the little bugger still remembers it twenty years later.

4. I enjoy boisterous kids, as long as it's not the little urchin kicking the back of my airline seat. Conversely, I worry about the children who act terrified and silent. What's wrong?

5. There are more than 250 million adults in the United States. Each one started as a baby and then grew up and moved out, so there's a high probability that yours will, too.

6. If you see another frustrated young mother with incorrigible kids (and you will), offer a smile, open a door, or say something pleasant to the child. That works so much better than snarling at the exhausted woman and ordering her to control her rotten brats. That action could prompt puke on your shoe. And not from the child.

It comes down to survival of the funniest. I know a young single mother who recently went through the checkout with only two items: diapers and wine. Thousands of older women would salute her and send encouragement. Someday she won't need to buy the diapers.

~

What the Hell Happened to My Body

Let's talk about Kegels, incontinence, and crazy caballeros. There's a reason most women past thirty don't ride on galloping horses, jump on trampolines, or finish a set of jumping jacks during exercise class. We wet our pants. Throw in a simple sneeze, and it's all over. The floor. Literally.

Even after years of faithfully doing Kegel exercises to strengthen pelvic floor muscles, we remain a bit fearful of spontaneous activities that require bladder control. We wouldn't dare wear white pants to jump rope with our grandkids, and lifting a sack of potatoes could ruin a good day at the market. For the two bored and bewildered men who may be reading this, a Kegel exercise involves contracting and releasing the muscles that stop urination. Tighter pelvic muscles help in other areas, too, but we'll discuss that another time.

According to the Agency for Healthcare Research and Quality, 35 percent of American middle-aged women experience urinary incontinence. That's more than 10 million people you should avoid sitting next to at a comedy show.

Most comedy clubs have easy access to the women's bathrooms because we love to laugh without needing to wear Depends. I've seen live shows by comediennes Rita Rudner, Joan Rivers, and Stacy Dymalski. After the performances, the women in the audience stampede to the restrooms like herds of wildebeests, ever ready to fall over the cliff of death rather than suffer the total humiliation of wet pants.

For some dry facts, the reasons for bladder control problems include pregnancy and childbirth, urinary tract infections, disease, some medications, injuries, and yep, old age. Doctors recommend several remedies: cut back on caffeine because it acts as a diuretic, always carry protective pads, schedule regular restroom breaks, consider hormone creams, try biofeedback techniques, use a support device, or ask about the 300 surgical options available to treat incontinence. There's always the Chinese therapy involving vaginal weights, which gives a whole new meaning to the term Chinese Take-Out. Finally, talk with other women who are successfully dealing with the issue. Prompt a lively discussion at your next society luncheon by asking, "Do you wet your pants every time you sneeze, cough, or laugh?"

We've all read articles about amazing middle-aged ballerinas and gymnasts who can still run and jump like manic gazelles, but they probably never gave natural birth to anyone larger than two pounds. Diana Nyad is a great example of an amazing middle-age athlete, but she swims across oceans, so during her sport she can just pee whenever she wants.

My children came with a force so powerful it should have been studied by NASA. And those industrial-sized cherubs altered every surrounding organ in their quest to leave my body. Even after corrective surgery to hoist and stitch everything back in place, I still don't trust a good belly laugh without checking for the nearest exit.

On a recent vacation in Mexico, Studley surprised me with an excursion to ride horses on the beach along the Pacific Ocean. He's heard my legendary stories about riding in the Gooding County Fair and Rodeo, and he knows I was a gallant barrel racer. As the decades passed, my story became more animated and grandiose. I had him convinced that my white horse was the greatest barrel racer that ever lived, when in reality she was an old gray mare that raced around barrels because there were sugar cubes at the end of the ride. I have adopted this philosophy throughout my life. I'll run fast if someone's making dessert.

His eyes positively glowed when he told me about the impending horseback ride on the beach. I didn't have the heart to tell him it had been more than twenty-five years since I last rode a horse, and wouldn't new jewelry be just as exciting?

We arrived for our ride and were handed huge lead-lined goblets of beer from a battered keg marked Cerveza Pacifico. Our horses eyed us with despair, but we quaffed our beers and wrangled onto the saddles. The first hour was fun as we galloped along the beach with our singing guide. Then my body realized it had endured all the fun it needed. By the second hour of trotting and galloping in the saddle, my bladder declared mutiny. I had to go NOW!

A few scraggly bushes offered the only privacy, and I had a real Charley horse in my leg. I knew that if I got down, there was only a 20 percent chance I'd ever get back up on the horse. So I meditated and practiced the Kegel exercises as Studley and the crazy caballero hooped and hollered on their rides. My horse was clearly irritated and commenced to relieve himself regularly, as if to mock my dire situation.

After what seemed like two weeks, we finally returned to the corrals. Both men had to help me down, and I waddled to the nearest fly-infested relief station as my horse eagerly trotted away. I'm sure the horses gather at the end of the day to commiserate about their riders.

"I suffered through a total jerk today. He kept kicking my sides to make me gallop, and you know how my bursitis is acting up these days."

"Well, I carried a soggy sissy who was afraid to let me run freely."

"Someday we'll blow this gig and settle down on some lush farm in Kentucky."

I truly appreciated my husband's loving gesture, but I hinted that for our next adventure we could attend a romantic musical at a fancy theatre with plush velour seats, a selection of fine wines, and several clean bathrooms reserved for women over forty-five. I hear a boisterous chorus shouting, "Amen, sister!"

Another example of body betrayal is the unstoppable migration of our sagging breasts. Long, long ago, these perky orbs were the well-rounded example of young womanhood, but now they're resting quietly near our elbows. They seem to be quite happy there and in no hurry to move back up where they belong unless we force them to be manipulated for the dreaded but necessary mammogram.

I usually schedule multiple appointments for a full-body tune-up and lube during the month of September. During the last round of visits, I was pricked, prodded, flossed, scoped, and dilated as nurses and doctors scribbled notes and muttered in amazement that someone so old could be so healthy. My biggest regret, besides stepping on the scale, was that I didn't bring along a full flask of cabernet.

During the procedure, I concentrated on the escape window as a sassy young nurse handled my breasts while muttering, "Damn, that's a lotta skin!"

"You need to apply these nipple stickers first," she said. "That's so the X-ray technicians can identify their location."

"I'm menopausal," I replied. "They can find my nipples somewhere down at my waist."

She wasn't amused and handed me two little stickers with tiny steel balls in the middle. I was instructed to apply them in the exact area and wait for further instructions. I imagined being a geriatric showgirl wearing miniscule pasties in an old-timer's burlesque show. The word "perky" wasn't part of the performance.

Finally she manipulated one nipple-decorated boob onto the plate and squeezed the clamp until my eyes watered. I watched in horror as my pummeled mammary oozed into the next room. I think I heard her cackle.

"Doing okay?" she chirped.

"Die, wench!" I gasped between clenched teeth.

She tortured one side for several X-rays and then moved to the other one, efficiently stretching, molding, and positioning my breast as if she were a celebrated sculptor. My brain was flooded with fight-or-flight signals as I resisted the temptation to knock over the offensive machine, tie up the nurse with the flaps of my flimsy gown, attack her face with nipple stickers, and run screaming from the building.

I was finalizing my plan when she announced that the procedure was completed.

"You're free to go," she said. "And don't forget to remove those nipple stickers."

She left me alone clutching my body with the swaying nipple ornaments. I ripped off the first sticker, which immediately caused guttural groans similar to the sounds I've heard on the National Geographic channel when a beast slaughters a wild hog. Some tender body parts aren't meant to wear super-glued decorations. I focused on a spot on the ceiling—a technique I used decades ago during the pains of childbirth—and tugged at the remaining sticker. It wouldn't detach. I was the victim of a nipple attack.

Mild panic consumed my mind and body. Should I go into the lobby and ask for help? Should I just be tough, get dressed, and hope the sticker would fall off in the shower? Should I go to the nearest bar and drink a bottle of wine? I gave one last pull, and the offensive nipple sticker came off, so I defiantly stuck it on the window, dressed, and hunched out of the office.

A few days later, my cell phone rang with the good news. "No signs of breast cancer! See you in a year." All the other medical tests came back positive, too, so I should be around to irritate people for many years. I am profoundly grateful for good health, but I'm still having flashbacks. My wee granddaughter recently asked if I had any stickers, and I started to whimper. She'll discover why in about thirty years.

I started wearing a bra at age ten when my other friends didn't have enough development to fill a Band-Aid. The double-Ds started dragging by my early thirties. Twenty seconds after I entered perimenopause, my boobs went from gravity-defying orbs that could be seen from outer space to unsightly tube socks lolling in my lap. Now only

industrial-strength fabric and high-powered hydraulic con-
traptions can hoist these babies above my elbows.

After forty years, breasts fall (yes, fall) victim to the realities of age and the consequences of pregnancy and nursing.
I use this information to make my adult children feel guilty.
Also, crazy hormones during menopause cause loss of full-
ness and painful tenderness.

I have used heating pads or warm water bottles to reduce
discomfort, and I wear a sturdy bra to keep the girls where
they belong. Regular exercise can help tone and tighten
sagging skin, and I tried lifting weights until I found one
hundred excuses to stop. Many women consider surgery
to lift and augment wandering breasts, but they should get
second and third opinions and weigh all the costs. What's
better—cutting into your chest or taking a trip to Europe?

I read that I could soothe breast tenderness with castor
oil, lavender essential oil, or natural progesterone cream. I
decided to turn the experiment into a potential for passion
and enlisted the help from a supportive partner to massage
the potions onto my skin. Who knew aging could be so
much fun?

There's something else I need to get off my chest. For
the past year, I've been fighting old age with the tenacity of
Wonder Woman, but the only thing we have in common
is the super-human bosom that means we can use our old
bras to cover the entire garden during an early freeze. We
don't have the same physique because the sand in my hour-
glass figure morphed into dunes complete with rolling hills
and hidden crevices. And lolling around in front of me are
boobs that could have fed the entire newborn unit at St.
Mark's Hospital in Salt Lake City.

Female athletes in the Olympics include amazing gymnasts, dancers, runners, and skiers who have the figures of twelve-year-old boys. Their intense exercise burns every extra ounce of fat, so apparently I'll never qualify for the team. Research shows that a double-D cup carries more than five pounds of additional weight. No wonder our racks hurt our backs. It's as if we're always toting a smoked ham hung from our shoulders.

I wanted to continue my exercise routine, so my trainer graciously took me to be fitted for a sports bra. The store had one that was large enough, and it cost $60. The contraption smashed everything so tight that my boobs were moved under my armpits. Not an attractive vision. With the assistance of two healthy women with Buick-lifting biceps, we spent several minutes tightening, binding, and harnessing the jugs until they were properly restrained. I could only breathe in tiny puffs of air, but I was relatively flat. It was amazing to actually look down and see my feet.

My new yoke made it easier to complete the workout sessions with the other svelte women. The problem came when I went home and removed the sports bra. My breasts flew out with a pent-up rage and hit the door, ironically becoming their own knockers.

At least the garment didn't resemble the first sports bra. In 1977, a group of women sewed two jock straps together and slung them over their shoulders. An earlier version of the original Jogbra is preserved at the Smithsonian. I don't want to wear any hybrid invention that started as a jock strap, so I'll sit in my recliner with a tub of ice cream and watch the Olympics.

Accepting my aging body allows me to tolerate sporadic episodes of humiliation and glorious crescendos of joy. In other words, a typical song in the life of a middle-aged woman. After all these years, I've learned to accept the fact that if I dare to venture into public, somehow I will embarrass myself.

For example, I went on a serious visit to City Hall with my son-in-law to finalize some business documents. Of course, I wanted to appear serious and intelligent, but as I stepped from the car, I noticed I was wearing my "chicken slippers," a delightful pair of comfortable slippers with a perky chicken on the left foot and a cracked egg with a peeking chick on the right foot. I wear these slippers around the house because I'm a recovering high-heeled-shoe addict with the bunions to prove it. In my haste to get to the meeting, I had completely forgotten to change my shoes. Was it a silent but sassy protest of city government bureaucracy? Probably not. Was it old-age confusion? Perhaps.

Another moment that ignited the wounded warrior within my aging soul happened when I eagerly went to the Boise Philharmonic to experience the world premiere of *An Idaho Symphony.* My perky mood turned as dark as the surrounding black-clothed patrons when the insensitive spawn-of-the-devil ticket taker asked if I wanted the senior citizen discount. Even though it was cheaper, I couldn't accept the erroneous assumption that I was six years older. I stumbled to my seat and sat in total despair until the orchestra turned my gloom to glee with a breathtaking rendition of Igor Stravinsky's *Firebird Suite.* Then the new symphony dedicated to Idaho restored my elation as it captured the mood and magnificence of the state.

Those glorious feelings evaporated about two seconds after I drove home in a snowstorm. A recent Idaho winter lasted about three years, so I packed my hide-all black swimsuit, new black sandals, and glue-on fake toenails and headed south to a spa near the ocean. (Sometimes I use fake toenails with sandals because my nails don't grow and my toes resemble ugly, chubby sausages. I fear that hungry rodents will burst from the bushes and snack on my feet.) Within the first hour at the resort, I accidentally stepped into a shallow pool of water, and the dye on the new sandals covered my feet in black and white stripes. Luckily, my fake nails didn't come off.

I had arranged for a massage the following day, and I didn't want to appear with clown feet, so I decided to walk along the beach and let the sand wear off the dye. The two-hour stroll erased some of the black stripes, but unfortunately I got a hideous burn from the intense sun. Then the humidity turned my hair into an uncontrollable bush of wire thick enough to hold my keys, a water bottle, and a salacious novel.

I arrived the next morning at the spa, greeted by gentle hostesses named Jasmine and Camilla. Once ensconced in a fluffy white robe, I was ushered to the waiting room where chimes were tinkling and scented candles glowed in the dim light. In front of me sat the most beautiful women I had ever seen. No, they didn't sit. They floated in the room with perfect skin, flawless faces, and tight, teeny bodies.

They turned in unison to stare as I stumbled into the room, tripped over the bamboo rug, spilled my mango-infused water, and lost two fake toenails. I sat there with a soaking robe, frizzy hair, black-striped feet, sunburned nose, and stubby toenails. As I retrieved the errant nails and stuffed them into my pocket, I knew that I had become the court jester in a room of Grecian goddesses.

But there's nothing like a ninety-minute massage to make all the mental and physical pains go away. The massage therapist applied scented oils to my sunburn, dug her elbows into my aching back, and rubbed my feet with soothing cream. By the end, I wanted to take her home with me. I happily glided back to my room, grateful to feel so good and eager for my next entertaining adventure.

My relaxing vacation was too short. I returned home to a multitude of messages and appointments, and the first one was an eye examination. I gathered my prescription eyeglasses, prescription sunglasses, contact lenses, and regular sunglasses and saw my way to the ophthalmologist.

"I think we need to do a test for macular degeneration," my eye doctor mumbled as he nonchalantly studied the results of my exam.

"Holy crap!" I responded, a bit more animated. "Am I going blind?"

Immediately, I feared the worst. How could I exist without seeing my grinning Studley bring me coffee every morning, or watch my extraordinary grandchildren blossom into exquisite youngsters, or visually feast upon the multiple splendors of outdoor Idaho? How would I know if my purse and shoes were coordinated? And, horrors, what if I accidentally opened a cheap chardonnay instead of a rich cabernet? The pending consequences were more than I could bear.

My thoughts were erupting like microwave popcorn as the perky assistant led me to a strange machine. She probably had 20-20 vision and secretly pitied my older, frightened eyes. I sat where instructed and placed my chin in the designated slot. "Just stare at the colored lines and don't blink for six seconds," she said. I have a three-second attention span, so it took four tries to get it right. Then we zapped the other eye. She left me alone with this mind-numbing remark: "It'll be just a minute, dear."

Dear? I was about to fall into a black abyss, and somehow this young stranger managed to make it worse. A tear wiggled out of my favorite eye (it's the left one). I began the Holy Barter, which is my term for promising the Spiritual Universe to do ANYTHING for another chance. My list went like this: I won't be on the computer for hours without a break. I'll get more sleep. I won't attempt to write 7,000 words in a weekend. I promise to wear my glasses, even in public! Just, please, don't take my vision.

I was ten years old when I put on my friend's glasses and realized that trees had leaves! Until then, trees were just big green things. Then I noticed that the teacher was writing actual words on the blackboard. No wonder I had been having trouble in school. After I finally got prescription glasses, we attended a movie, and I cried like a baby because I could actually see that Bambi was all alone in the forest!

Since then, my eye problems have included ulcers, floaters, and painful night vision. When I was twenty-five and pregnant with my first child, my vision became blurry. I thought I couldn't see the scales because of my huge belly, but my ophthalmologist confirmed that I had holes in my retinas. Immediate surgery was required, but I refused anesthesia because of the pregnancy. Nothing prompts projectile vomiting more than seeing your own eyeball manipulated and welded. After the bandages were removed, I was relieved that my vision was good enough to find the sales rack at Nordstrom's.

All these thoughts were whirling through my feeble mind as I waited for the eye doctor to say the words that would either send me into chaotic darkness or make me fall on my knees and celebrate the everlasting lightness of being and seeing. I held my breath as the doctor entered the room, read the charts, and uttered these profound words:

"Your eyes are weaker, and there is some deterioration of the lining, but you don't have macular degeneration. You just have old eyeballs."

I stifled the urge to both hit and kiss him. It's just old eyeballs! Alleluia! I could see well enough to order new glasses, pay the migraine-inducing bill, and drive without assistance. On my way home, I noticed an abandoned car rusting in a field and decided I wasn't ready for the scrap-yard. I promised myself that I would keep a regular maintenance schedule that included eye and dental exams, pap smears, and mammograms. I wanted to enjoy my golden years without too much tarnish, and I could see clearly that getting dull was not an option.

Recently, I literally redefined the term "old farts." The good news: I lost a few pounds in a few hours. The bad news: a stranger inserted a camera at least a mile up my butt, and then she charged me $1,500 for the privilege. The doctor said not to drink alcohol for twenty-four hours after the procedure, but I was swilling wine five minutes after I limped into the house, farting with every step.

Because I am over fifty years old and want to live long enough to irritate my great-grandchildren, I advocate regular exercise and preventive medicine. And for middle-aged women, that includes having regular mammograms that smash your boobs between the jaws of death, pap smears from a cheerful young nurse who wants to chat while all you can see is her perky head, and now colonoscopies, a probing expedition in search of rear-end damage.

Here are the sobering facts: 1 in 19 people will be diagnosed with colon cancer in their life, and 1 in 45 will die from it. I have 626 friends on Facebook, so that means thirteen will die from colon cancer. It's curable if found early. Do I have your attention now?

The day before the procedure, you need to consume only clear liquids. Red wine is not included on this list. In the evening, swallow a gallon of thick liquid that tastes and looks like buffalo snot mixed with mouse droppings. Then you gather books, cell phone, and computer and retire to the bathroom where you'll spend the night recreating the bathroom scene from the movie *Dumb and Dumber.*

This experience will test and/or strengthen your love life. Throughout the Evening of Gurgling Misery, Studley brought me popsicles and hid the wine openers. He offered amazing tidbits of information, such as did I know the average colon is between five and six feet long? Did I know the colon can store up to ten pounds of processed food per foot? After an hour of fascinating facts, I told him where to put his research.

On the Day of the Invasion, I needed a designated driver, so Studley discreetly placed a waterproof pad in the passenger seat before he took me to the clinic. But we both knew I would jump out in the middle of congested traffic on State Street before I'd mess up his new pickup truck. And

I promise to return the favor when it's time for his procedure. Love works that way.

At the clinic, I was given a wonderful sedative and wheeled into The Room. I was joking with the doctor about getting a bull's eye painted so it would be easier for her… and then suddenly I woke up in recovery. I was in a room full of cubicles with other post-op patients, and everyone was passing gas. That's because air is pumped inside the colon so the camera can be maneuvered on its incredible voyage of discovery, and then the air needs to get back out. I couldn't stop laughing at the Old Fart version of the campfire scene in *Blazing Saddles*.

Despite the inconvenience, I encourage all my friends over fifty to schedule colonoscopies. You won't be photographed at your best angle, but I don't want to stand up at your funeral and yell, "I told you so!" I need all the friends I can get, so please endure two days of humiliation in order to survive and grow old with me so we can shuffle together into the closest wine bar.

It's been said that a woman's hair is her crowning glory. Mine is frizzy and thin, so I need to rent a wig before I can feel glorious. I have no clue how gray my hair is because I've dyed it for more than twenty years. If I ever lapse into a long coma, after a few months no one will recognize the old gray-haired lady sleeping in my bed. I've tried several times to let it go natural, but after two months the ravaged result is so pitiful that I go back to the bottle. And then I also get another bottle of dye.

My hair salon offered a holiday special that included a free upper lip wax with any regular service. Being in a festive mood after my haircut, I gleefully agreed and prepared for my face to be smooth as a baby's butt. Instead, the pretty young hairdresser plastered enough hot wax to remove Geraldo Rivera's mustache, and when she ripped it off, the wax tore off patches of skin from my tender lip. I was left with bloody scabs just in time for important year-end meetings and jolly Christmas parties.

"I'm so sorry," she gushed as she smeared Vaseline across the ravaged lip. "Your lip is so thin some wax accidentally smeared over it."

So now she had inflicted bodily harm AND insulted my features. (I love my lip because it's the only thin thing on my body.) I looked around for a hot curling iron to shove up her nose, but my eyes were tearing too much to see clearly. Instead, I did what most women do: I said it was okay. Why in the hell did I say that? It wasn't okay. I was in breathless pain, and blood was oozing from my greasy lip.

She still needed to style my hair, so she handed me the latest issue of *Cosmopolitan* magazine and offered me a cup of coffee. I snarled no because I didn't want to plunge my battered mouth into steaming hot liquid. She turned on the blow dryer, and I anticipated she would set my hair on fire to make me forget the pain in my lip.

The perfect faces in the magazine only taunted my hapless predicament. I flipped to an article titled "52 Hot Crazy Sex Moves." One suggestion to ignite my inner sex kitten was to spank my lover with a paddle that left heart-shaped marks on his butt. Why would I do that? To make him forget my abused mouth? My inner sex kitten would rather have some milk and take a nap, and Studley would prefer a sandwich and a cold beer.

Another provocative article discussed the serious topic of sex toys and endorsed a vibrator shaped like a candy cane. I often have small grandchildren running around the house, so I immediately erased the image of them finding such a device and happily bringing it to the holiday dining table for all the guests to see. Turn the page, turn the page.

As a writer, I often wonder who writes the trash in women's magazines. Some writer actually pitches a ridiculous story and gets paid to write it. Maybe I should submit an article titled "Hot Crazy Sex Moves for Those over 50." I'll bet a month's supply of iron tablets and stool softener pills that it would get rejected.

Cosmopolitan magazine has been published since 1886 and has paid subscriptions from 3 million readers. It has sixty-four international editions printed in thirty-five languages and is distributed to more than a hundred countries, including Mongolia. The temperature there is now 22 degrees. The natives are so bundled in warm clothes that a swat on the butt with a seductive paddle wouldn't be noticed. Maybe I could write an article about how to get pleasure by sending your hairdresser to Mongolia. I'd laugh, but that would hurt.

~

Blending Fine Wine
and Vintage Friends

I frequently experience brilliant bouts of understanding, clarity, and truth after consuming a glass or two of red wine. The bolder the wine, the wiser and more enlightened I become. After a really good bottle, I am a freakin' maharishi.

With great gusto and energetic enthusiasm, I have contributed to the growth and success of the wine industry because I enjoy meeting friends for a drink (or bottle) of wine. It's a duty I willingly accept as part of my mission to help stimulate the economy. I should receive a plaque from the local Chamber of Commerce, but a case of wine would be better.

My mother often shared a pot of Maxwell House coffee with her friends, and she would decorate the table with matching china and dainty napkins. A really special friend would be offered pastel mints in a crystal bowl. They would sip their drinks, share meatloaf recipes, and murmur about how the music of The Beatles came straight from Satan. I observed these rituals with a sense of wonder and confusion and never was offered any pastel mints.

I didn't have time for morning coffee klatches when I was juggling young children and a career. Home-brewed coffee in a travel mug got me to work, and the habit sustained me for several decades. Life got better with age, and then the kids got older. I no longer worked full-time, and I discovered that no, I wasn't Super Woman, and I'd rather lift a wine glass than a briefcase. Who knew? I'd been climbing the corporate ladder in heels when I should have been sashaying in perky sandals to meet friends at the nearest wine bar.

One benefit of being this old is that I have friends who range in age from their twenties to their seventies. We meet for a glass of wine to celebrate important events, such as if the sun came up again. Instead of swapping stories about meatloaf recipes, we analyze a variety of topics from modern literature to midlife libido. In a typical week, I'll juggle six appointments to meet different friends, including a thirty-five-year-old with two small children and several jobs, a forty-year-old divorced woman with a court victory, a fifty-year-old with teenagers and her own business, and a fifty-nine-year-old friend I've known since 1968. Another one is a bleeding-heart liberal, and yet another thinks the country is doomed and is stocking canned soup. Still, we meet, share laughs, clink our wine glasses, and order another round. And, as I remember from the Maxwell House commercials, it's always good to the last drop.

My friends are like colorful pieces in a marvelous tapestry. Some are from my college days, others are in a group of women who worked at a corporation in Boise, a few are neighbors, and the rest are assorted acquaintances, volunteers, and miscellaneous friends that come and go like a favorite old song. I've noticed that lately some of them are looking rather ragged, and there are days I'd like to be hung from a quilt rack just to help smooth out the wrinkles.

I recently attended a tea party with a dozen feisty middle-aged women. It was too early for wine (so they said), so we sat in a friend's garden sipping tea from her mother's ornate tea set. We all once worked for the same corporation, and as our lives have evolved, most of us are still jumping in and out of hot water when we should be lolling around on the patio receiving a massage from a bodybuilder named Thor.

Linda was widowed after her husband died unexpectedly. Determined to take care of herself, she closed up their winter Arizona home and drove by herself back to Idaho. She arrived at 1:30 in the morning, only to discover she didn't have the key to open the door.

"It was always *his* job to do that!" she explained.

Exhausted after the thirteen-hour drive, she did what any resourceful woman would do. She took a hammer from the tool box in her car and broke down the door.

"It felt great!" she said. "I got rid of a lot of pain."

Another friend, Sue, described how she was petitioning the court for guardianship of her teenage granddaughter because of the mother's chronic drug abuse problems. "We were all set to enjoy our retirement," she said. "Now we have a teenager in the house. But, we'll make it work."

One of my oldest friends, and I mean old by the number of years we've been acquainted, is Carol. She announced that she has developed heart disease, the number-one cause of death for women. We immediately shared hugs and started to wait on her every need. She remarked that she should have mentioned the disease years earlier. She's doing fine, but her health alarm is a reminder that life is fragile and getting older is a privilege denied to many others.

"Stop having heart disease," I said. "I don't want to feel guilty about all the wild times we've had together. We left the corporate rat race, and now we deserve to sit by the pool in colorful outfits and whistle for more drinks."

She nodded in agreement. "I'll meet you poolside anytime. But, we'll alternate libations with lemon water."

Another friend told us about being diagnosed with Type 2 diabetes. We encouraged her to take care of herself, and then we arm-wrestled her to remove the cookies from her reach.

"If we aren't allowed to enjoy an abundance of sweets, why do cookies come by the dozen?" she lamented. We shook our heads in communal sympathy.

I tried to lighten the mood by describing how my elderly mother burned up her microwave by using it as a timer and then unknowingly gave my daughter a toy that spewed recorded obscenities. We weren't making fun of her because we knew we'll probably be doing the same things in twenty years.

A few women described the challenges of caring for a sick parent. We traded suggestions, anecdotes, and recommended care facilities. Most of us had lost at least one parent, and the surviving spouse was alone. Except for Sue's mother who is known as the incurable flirt at her retirement center. We decided to copy that example.

After listening to each other's circumstances, we agreed that we would make the most out of the last third of our lives. Molly announced that she was resigning from her job after working for thirty-four years and was planning her retirement. We toasted her with vanilla tea and poppy seed cake. One woman was eagerly anticipating the birth of her first grandchild. The other grandmothers in the group all chimed in on the wonders of being a grandmother. Of course, we all pulled out photographs and declared that the world would be a better place because of our perfect progeny.

For over twenty years, we've shared the highs and lows of our interesting and varied lives. Sometimes it takes a cozy tea party in an elegant garden to renew our spirits before returning to the real world for the next challenge. As we left the party, we all vowed to carry a hammer, just in case we had to bust down a door.

Another group of feisty friends over forty invited me to join them for dinner and the movie *Sex and the City*. I rarely watched the show on television, so I was expecting a pandering, plotless portrayal of bed-hopping bimbos. I was pleasantly surprised. The movie was fun, and it included just the right amount of bold sass and bare ass.

After the movie, three of our group went home to husbands, and four went home alone. Of those four, one was recently widowed, two were divorced, and one was separated from her husband. The variety and reality of our lives didn't matter. We enjoyed the evening and weren't shocked at images that would have sent our mothers into counseling and confession. We've come a long way from our first "skin" movie, *The Graduate* with a fresh-faced Dustin Hoffman. Those were the innocent times when we were left with the power of our imaginations.

For another movie date, we saw *Miss Pettigrew Lives for a Day* at the Flicks in Boise. (I love the Flicks because you can have wine and popcorn during the movie.) The movie was delightful; the fun plot included rewards for the "older woman" (finally!), and there was no blood, profanity, or gratuitous pandering. And, no twerking!

Five of the liveliest and oldest pieces in my friendship quilt include a group of women who met as college freshman at the University of Idaho more than forty years ago. For Shreve, Kitty, Bonin, Jennifer and me, freedom was new and intoxicating, and we discovered that the uncharted life away from our parents was best shared with good friends.

We were the first generation of career women. Our mothers didn't work outside the home, and we had few role models for working women, so we pulled up our big-girl pants and figured out what to do. Now, at the end of our careers, we can relax and turn to other important issues, such as cabernet and colonoscopies.

All six of us graduated from the University of Idaho, three earned master's degrees, and one has a PhD. We worked in professional careers while balancing marriages, children, homes, and volunteer activities. We have twelve children—all gainfully employed—and we can proudly boast that not one has been in jail or starred in a television reality show. We all have daughters, and our main advice to them was: be able to support yourself. And be nice to your friends because someday they could write a book and include you.

We worked when there were few childcare options, and we survived on five hours of sleep a night. After a day's work, we fed and bathed our children, read them stories, tucked them into bed, and then we did white laundry on Monday, dark laundry on Tuesday, sheets and towels on Wednesday, and bought groceries on Thursday. We juggled piano lessons, Little League, and teacher conferences without a cell phone or computer. We paved the way as mentors for younger women, and we didn't demand a thank you note.

We have shared the significant experiences of our weddings, pregnancies, and the death of parents. Four of us have been married more than thirty years to the original husband. Thirty percent have been divorced and remarried, and they are 100 percent happy about that. Now the grandchildren are arriving, and we're already planning their future marriages to each other. We all have different political and religious beliefs, but that's secondary to our main truth: we are true friends.

During our brief reunion, we laughed ourselves silly while consuming copious quantities of cabernet and platters piled with decadent desserts. We reflected on our lives, shared our stories, and commiserated about health issues. Yes, we will endure those horrible colonoscopies and mammograms because we want to live long enough to enjoy more parties. We intend to march boldly into old age and tell any detractors to kiss our attitudes. And we'll never forget the day we rushed into the Delta Gamma sorority in Moscow, Idaho, and loudly proclaimed, "We are sisters."

Though we've never lived in the same towns, we have continued to get together. When our kids were little, we enjoyed family slumber parties, float trips on the river, and vacations at a mountain lodge. After our kids got older, we enjoyed women-only trips. To celebrate our 55th birthdays, we traveled to Maui, to hike across a volcano, savor spa treatments, and watch the sun rise over the ocean.

Last year, we met in San Francisco to attend the wedding of one of our daughters. We arrived at the Oakland airport, all wearing sensible shoes and black pants suits while rolling our eyes at the young ladies hobbling about on stiletto heels. We are seasoned travelers through life, and we tossed the heels many years ago.

As we shared coffee and laughs while waiting for the shuttle bus into the city, we planned how we would sing to the bride at the reception, just as we did back at the Delta Gamma sorority and at every DG wedding since then. Some of the more sophisticated guests at the prestigious Fort Mason venue would be shocked at our exuberant antics, but as usual, we didn't give a rip.

Over our five-day mini-reunion, we laughed at the same stories, reminisced about our lives, and proved that a woman is never too old to throw off her shoes and joyfully dance at a wedding. We ate too much good food, drank too many delightful drinks, and visited too many wineries. But we also visited the gym in the hotel so we could stay fit enough to continue to party. We concluded that we could have one glass of wine for every ten minutes on the treadmill. There is absolutely no scientific evidence to validate that assumption, but we decided to not sweat the small stuff.

We've known the bride since she was a baby, and our wish is that her life will be full of passion, laughter, and good friends. During the inevitable bad times, she'll need her friends more than ever. We can be there in a few hours, and we promise to sing and dance until the sun comes up again. We know how to do that.

I adore my friends, and not one of them is crabby. The best way to sap the last sorry drop of vitality out of my aging spirit is to hang out with grumpy people. I appreciate the wisdom, counsel, and rich stories from positive older acquaintances, and I try to empathize with the poignant sadness of some older folks, but I also really enjoy an energy buzz from jumping into the chaotic creativity of younger people. I'm eager to share my knowledge and skills while I can still remember our names and maneuver a wine opener without hurting myself. It's a delicate achievement not to appear like the crazy old aunt in *Arsenic and Old Lace* or the tortured character of Norma Desmond in *Sunset Boulevard*. But as long as there are stories to write, songs to sing, and wine to enjoy, I'm choosing the team with the upstart rebels and young dreamers. Some day in the distant future when I'm content to sit in a rocker with a spill-proof sippy cup of wine, I hope a new generation of mentors will appear to collaborate with a group of feisty young artists. That's the best way to stay young at heart.

After I returned from the fun weekend with sorority sisters, I collapsed on the patio to sip a lovely merlot. A neighbor came over to share a glass, and she took a photo of me sipping wine. I posted the photo on Facebook, and then I almost deleted the photo because it made my face look haggard and horrible. And ghastly. It could be copied as a Halloween mask. It showed a mass of lines around my eyes that resembled the tangled roads on a cluttered cross-country map, crevices around my mouth that were deep enough to store pencils, and bulging bags underneath my eyes that proved it's a miracle I can even see. Yes, the photo sucked.

Blame it on the wine, but I decided not to delete the photo because I suddenly acknowledged a raw reality: I'm old.

Not old in the feeble way, but old because of the rich abundance of life experiences. The lines around my eyes have been etched by years of laughter mixed with a few painful periods of tears. Not even the most expensive creams can erase or hide six decades of emotions, joys, and sorrows that I carry like a telltale billboard on my face. It would be nice to hear someone declare, "Wow! That woman sure had a lot of laughter in her life!" That's SO much better than hearing the line about "rode hard and put away wet."

In another libation-induced moment of monumental awakening, I remembered that I'm not the center of the universe and it really doesn't matter a twit how many wrinkles wander over my chubby cheeks. It's rather liberating to finally endure a photograph of me as a woman who loves and accepts her vintage laugh lines. I earned them. Every damn one of them. And today I'm alive at least one more day to go out and earn some more.

To celebrate my new acceptance, I did what only comes naturally. I opened another bold cabernet, toasted the universe, and invited some friends to come over. Since ancient times, joyful people have shared wine to celebrate important events. I have enhanced that tradition. I'll drink fine wine if my hangnail heals.

～

Enlightenment After the Age of Aquarius

I'm often asked to give keynote speeches to various groups because I have a gift for bullshit and I can use finger puppets to make even the crabbiest person laugh for a few minutes. Every public speaker has inevitable worries: Will they laugh at my jokes? Do they understand three-syllable words? Am I going to have explosive diarrhea?

My biggest fear is not knowing who will be in the audience. Will it be that pesky groupie who always asks me how to get published—right now! Will it be Cousin Thomas who will tell me I'm going to hell if I don't change my ways? Or will it be THAT PERSON—the one who stabbed me in the back, kicked me in the gut, and pushed me off the corporate ladder more than twenty years ago? Yeah, I'm still hurt. And bitter. And wimpy enough to admit it.

Recently I was the keynote speaker at a prestigious event in southern Idaho. I got to the podium, looked out, and saw THAT PERSON. Instantly, the lower intestine began to gurgle so I automatically calculated the time and distance I needed to sprint to the bathroom. I feared that if I began to speak, some ancient Aztec curse would emerge and then my voice would sound like Darth Vader from *Star Wars*.

"I feel a tremor in the Force. The last time I felt it was in the presence of my old master. Don't underestimate the Force."

But maturity, common sense, and the desire to be paid for the speech overcame my momentary physical and mental disorders. I recovered my composure and no longer felt the need to fantasize that a giant, flying, prehistoric pterosaur would suddenly swoop into the room, snatch THAT PERSON, and fly away to feed hungry babies. No, it's been two decades, and I'm finally over it. I made eye contact, smiled, and increased the intensity of my presentation to give a stellar performance.

I know it's useless to carry a grudge, especially for twenty years. Letting go is liberating because why should I allow someone else to live rent-free in my head? Certain images of revenge against THAT PERSON do make for delicious short stories, which I have written and published, but the pain isn't as raw anymore because the wound is healed. I now can move on to satirize other irritating people. Besides, my life is abundant, and THAT PERSON looks sad and worn. Sweet.

I enjoy giving speeches to various groups of audiences eager for diversion and enlightenment with a spattering of humor. This causes great amusement and skepticism among my friends. A recent speech was at a meeting of 150 college coeds from the University of Idaho and Washington State University. It was a bit intimidating to be the wrinkled crone in the midst of such youth, beauty, and brilliance. I formulated the speech as I drove over 300 miles from Boise to Pullman, Washington.

Using the analogy of preparing for the journey of life, I talked about how we all get prepared for the trip: gas in the car, coat, toothbrush, etc., but we still don't know what obstacles we'll face before arriving at the final destination. Sure enough, I encountered horrible weather, complete with snow, freezing sleet, rain, and slush. But every so often, the clouds parted, and the sun broke through to reveal majestic mountains and blankets of snow that sparkled like sheets of diamonds.

I was playing my favorite music—Sarah Brightman, Il Divo, Latin Jazz, Bette Midler, and a collection of movie tunes. Driving through the Idaho mountains while listening to the theme song from *Out of Africa* can be a spiritual experience. But the attitude gets downright defiant when Bette starts belting out "I'm Beautiful, Damn it!" I had to use cruise control on that one, or I'd have been driving ninety miles an hour and flown right off the Whitebird Grade.

Just a few miles from my destination, I was getting eager for the six-hour trip to end. Then some idiot passed me on a hill, almost driving me off the road and spraying gravel and slush on the car. And there I was without a cannon attached to the hood so I could blast the rude pest from the road! Ironically, at the first stoplight I was directly behind the obnoxious punk. I had two choices: ram the back of his car, rip him out onto the road, and stomp on his ugly head—or laugh.

Wisely, I chose to laugh. He was just a kid and had decades ahead of him to worry about jobs, careers, family, and how to drive with sanity. I, on the other hand, had survived too many decades to fret about such youthful concerns.

The speech fell into place, and I talked about our journeys and the paths we take. Yes, there will be crap, stress, irritating people, and pain, but there will also be brilliant and breathtaking moments of success, beauty, anticipation, and glory. These young women seemed amazed that someone so incredibly old could actually speak without drooling or belching. I saved that for the trip home.

Some of my speeches require pomp and circumstance beyond my normal carefree demeanor. Even though I only have a bachelor's degree, I've been the commencement speaker at several colleges and universities. One of them may or may not have been Yale. That statement is entirely true. For the dignified procession, I wear a flowing robe and a velvet hat and ignore the smirks of those with PhDs who scoff at me because they're wearing different and nobler attire. I walk slowly as the orchestra plays, and nobody knows who I am. They just hope my talk will be brief.

At the last commencement speech, I told the graduates that they were doomed, there weren't any jobs, the country was teetering on the brink of destruction, they'll never get out of debt, and they should move into a tent in the forest and make macramé hangers to sell at craft fairs. Too harsh?

I regaled them with true but ancient anecdotes from my childhood. I grew up in a small town during an easier time. My mother would send me alone to the grocery store, and I would return with fresh bread, local eggs, a roast, and a pie or two. You can't do that anymore because stores expect to be paid at the time of purchase and you can't promise that mom will bring the money at the end of the month.

Thousands of graduates and their families sat through the commencement ceremonies, and I intently shared a few tidbits of wisdom while desperately searching for eye contact. It's difficult for motivational speakers to keep going when they know the audience already has checked out. So, while they were still awake, I eagerly preached my ten simple suggestions for a good life:

- **Accept the fact that life isn't fair.** You could work hard, excel at your job, and not be given time off to see your kid's school programs, only to see some pretty woman have an affair with the senior vice president and be given your job. Or you could get hit by a beer truck, or your spouse could run away with a carnival worker, or your hillbilly neighbor could get a lucrative reality show on television. Just change your profession and write country/western songs.

- **No one owes you a living.** Chances are you're not going to win the Publishers Clearing House Sweepstakes or the million-dollar lottery. And you can't live with your parents anymore because they want to buy a recreational vehicle and travel around to casinos. Go into the world and make your own way, one feisty step at a time.

- **Don't waste youthful energy and optimism.** Young college students should pursue their most elaborate goals and experience true freedom before life gives them a mortgage, kids, in-laws, fifty extra pounds, buffoon bosses, and irritable bowel syndrome.

- **Mansions, fast cars, and luxury vacations don't guarantee happiness.** Many good people are honestly delighted to have a small house with indoor plumbing, a pickup truck that runs, and a favorite camping place. Be like that.

- **Get out of debt.** Why work your entire life just to pay interest to a bank? In most cases, that $100 debt on your credit card for that sassy pair of boots will remain long after they have worn out. Pay cash or go bootless.

- **Enjoy relationships.** The happiest people are surrounded by family members and friends who accept their faults, celebrate their achievements, and invite them over for barbecues and wine. You may need to establish rules of engagement, such as no discussions about politics, religion, or who gets Grandma's good silverware after she dies.

- **Avoid crabby people.** They will suck out every last ounce of your energy and leave you a withered, bitter shell of wretched humanity. Purge your contact list now before it's too late.

- **Don't fight.** No explanation needed.

- **Love more.** Ditto.

- **Laugh, dance, and sing.** Triple ditto. Oh, and read more books.

I purposely avoided any mention of politics or religion because I'd rather crawl into a pit of poisonous snakes than tiptoe through the mine field of political correctness. For commencement speeches in May, I offer one last bit of advice: On Mother's Day, call your mom and thank her for putting up with you. If she is no longer living, call another mother and wish her a happy day. You'll both feel good.

Being around college graduates makes me an advocate for continuing education. In a bold attempt to spark my brain, a few years ago I participated in a live online class presented by Oprah and the author of the book *A New Earth—Awakening to Your Life's Purpose.* I decided to sign up for the class because I'm curious to know if my life's purpose involves more than driving fast, telling stories, and drinking red wine. Besides, I'm starting to worry about this age thing; I feel like I'm treading water in the deep and desperate end of the age pool, my body is falling apart, and my brain can't remember the ingredients for a BLT.

The first class took about ninety minutes, so I poured a glass of wine and settled in with my copy of the book and the worksheets while Eckhart Tolle, the author, explained some profound facts, such as "Worry pretends to be necessary, but serves no useful purpose." I was contemplating his words and was on the verge of one of Oprah's "ah-ha" moments when he started talking about the ego.

"Your ego lives in a constant state of not enough. The ego makes us over-eat, over-spend, and over-indulge." Instead of being enlightened, I was convicted. Why was he talking about me? I sipped my wine and pondered his words.

Then Oprah took a call from a woman in Berlin who claimed that the book had saved her life and helped her to stop drinking so much wine. My immediate reaction was to demand a refund for the class, take my wine, and walk out. But I didn't have to pay for it, and I was already home, so I kept listening.

The author extolled the virtues of consciously enjoying a single glass of wine every now and then. Only one at a time! Every now and then! That's like eating one M&M! Or one potato chip! Who can do that?

Well, by the end of the class I had a better understanding of the author's advice. Here are some of his other statements:

eat rude people as royalty and then watch them change." "The primary moment in your life is NOW. Accept it as it is." "Some people are addicted to the energy of unhappiness. Ego loves drama."

These statements make me think—so much that it hurt my brain. I had to let it rest and go have only one more glass of wine. (He didn't say how big the glass could be, so maybe I used a glass mixing bowl. But I contemplated and savored the experience and consciously enjoyed every indulgent sip.)

After struggling with the attempt at enlightenment, I decided to just accept my comfortable older body and go eat cookies. No one expects perfection because there isn't any.

As another piece of profound wisdom, I know that one of the best reasons to slide gleefully down the backside of middle age is to reach that glorious oasis where I just don't care anymore if my socks match, or if my plastic pink flamingo in the yard irritates the neighbors, or if I could braid the twig-sized hairs growing out of my chin. My life is an inviting place that reminds me of my paternal grandmother's old rocking chair, the one with the sagging, butter-soft, leather seat and the wooden arms worn white with wear. Finally, I'm comfortable with where and who I am.

Every now and then I scowl at teenagers with pants hanging below their butts. I ask others with shaggy, multicolored hair if their parent was a parrot. I audibly gasp at baristas with multiple piercings in their lips, noses, and eyebrows and angry tattoos crawling up both arms. And I've been known to roll down my window and tell the gyrating rebels in the next car to turn down the heavy metal music because it's peeling the paint from my car. They can't hear me, of course, because they're going deaf.

I vaguely remember back in the dark ages when I was young. There were plenty of old farts telling me, "Cut your bangs," or, "Turn down that gawd-awful music!" Obviously, I irritated the mature crowd when I was young, but now I've switched places. I try not to mutter as I encounter this generation's crop of dudes and divas but my hair didn't resemble a mixture of spilled, Day-Glo paint plastered rigid with super glue. And the music of The Beatles and the Beach Boys seems nursing-home tame compared to the jet-engine shrill of today's harsh sounds that could be used to torture prisoners into confessing that they ate the body of Jimmy Hoffa.

Maybe it's inevitable to turn into the image of the old lady with the purse from the 1968 television show *Laugh-In*. I should just go sit on a park bench and wait for an elderly man to shuffle up and offer me a Walnetto. (A favorite *Laugh-In* skit.) Except now, I'd probably take the Walnetto and tell him to hit the road. Because, at my age, I can say anything I want.

One of the many advantages of living in the last third of life is that I don't accept crap from anyone. I wasted valuable time during my thirties and forties posing as a pleaser, forever scampering around to ensure that everyone was happy while concurrently fighting manic hormones that were yelling at me to break something. Now, like a fine wine aged to perfection, I just don't give a rip.

Facebook periodically presents a trap that I fall into if I'm not vigilant about keeping my comments sassy and humorous. One time, an associate who just happens to be a politician made a comment on Facebook. I added a factual statement that provided an alternative opinion. Holy

Hot Flash! Suddenly, strangers wrote comments suggesting that I was stupid and wrong. One challenged me by name to check my facts. Another threw in an entire paragraph of questions and demanded that I answer them. These hostile comments received "like" comments from other strangers who don't know me.

Of course, feeling threatened, defensive, and unjustly attacked, I wrote and posted an excellent rebuttal that factually substantiated my original post. Then I waited. No one "liked" my rebuttal. Obviously, nobody wanted an intelligent debate. Sigh. So I decided, once again, that it is impossible for some groups to engage in civil discourse and show tolerance for diversity of opinion. I removed all my posts to this person, un-friended the one person I knew who "liked" the attacks on me, and placed a hammer on my desk. I taped a note on the hammer that reads: *Use this to hit head instead of making another political comment on Facebook.*

Humorist Erma Bombeck once wrote that guilt was the gift that keeps on giving. I no longer want this gift because it makes me crabby, unproductive, and resentful when I prefer to be sparkling, positive, and somewhat creative. So I intend to scamper to the top of this heavy pile of baggage, raise my liberated, wrinkled arms to the sky, and declare with gusto: Guilt be gone!

I started carrying bags of guilt when I returned to work full-time and my children, ages two and five, went to ten hours of childcare five days a week. Back in the pioneer days of Women in Management, businesses did not offer flex time, time off for birthday parties at school, or tolerance for sick children. "Suck it up and get to work" was the prevailing philosophy.

I started to shed the guilt when my darling children went off to college, just about the same time my widowed mother's health began to decline. She lived alone for twenty years before I moved her to an assisted living facility in Boise. After each visit, she would sit in her wheelchair in the doorway of her apartment and wave until I was out of sight. The baggage came back.

To preserve what remains of my eroding sanity, I refuse to pick up the bags again. I take comfort in knowing that my children are wonderful young adults who are making the world a better place. They are happily married, and their homes are full of love. We see my mother more than ever, and we include her in our family activities. So, get behind me, Guilt, because I'm not going to carry your bags anymore. Now my garbage will consist of empty wine bottles.

To finalize our discussion about enlightenment, let's consider a small piece of clothing that possesses entirely too much power over our self-confidence: the swimsuit.

We survived another swimsuit season without accidentally pushing some bikini-clad beauty into the pool! Hooray for us! After all these years, most middle-aged marvels have finally outgrown the suit and the trepidation about wearing it in public. Still, given the opportunity to lounge by a pool, some women would rather suffer acute diarrhea while driving through rush-hour traffic in an old van full of screaming toddlers and surly teenagers. Mature liberation takes time.

After years of wasted angst and black cover-ups, I've discovered a handy technique for dealing with the intimidating scenarios of the lifelong swimsuit competition: Laugh out loud. With gusto.

Pretty people at posh pools don't laugh. They grimace with exaggerated aloofness while dangling perfectly pedicured toes into the water and signaling for the dutiful wait staff to bring another cold beverage with an extra twist of organic lemon. If you pull the short straw and find yourself surrounded by such characters, just begin to giggle and then graduate into a boisterous guffaw until you reach hysterical laughter. Either they will join the fun or leave, so it's a win-win situation.

Recently, my husband and I celebrated our anniversary at a resort in Napa Valley. After a devoted day of tasting copious quantities of cabernet, we donned our respectable suits and sauntered to the adult pool. The last two empty chairs were wedged next to a gathering of young models covered with only two inches of material. My husband tried in vain to hide his approval. The only men for me to appreciate were old guys with their trophy women or the hairy-backed Europeans in Speedos.

Here are five tips for how to survive the next swimsuit season:

1. Grab your sweetie, get into the pool, and swim, laugh, and hug each other. Peek at the shocked and jealous glamour girls whose skimpy suits have never been wet.

2. Splash back to your chair, slather lotion over your well-seasoned body, order drinks, and laugh some more. It will drive others crazy.

3. Appreciate your body—the wrinkled eyes that have seen a lifetime of experiences, the wider hips that have carried strong babies, the age-spotted hands that have

dried tears and prayed for peace, and the soft lap that has rocked precious grandchildren.

4. Pull your sweetheart close, tousle his gray hair, and whisper a silly joke. Then laugh together until you snort.

5. Repeat 1 through 4.

The undisputable fact about growing older is that it happens or else we die young. Given those choices, I'll take the unknown opportunities of another year. I'll complete regular maintenance checkups, exercise, eat well, and laugh with intention. And I'll toast the memory of friends and relatives who didn't have the chance.

I'm grateful every autumn because it's time to put away the swimsuits, sandals, and silly insecurities, and bring out the sweaters and jeans. Then I order pizza and beer for dinner, and there can be donuts for breakfast. After all, I have several months to prepare for next summer.

~

Observing the Daze in Holidays

After a few decades, the holidays seem to merge from one box of jumbled decorations to the next. When my kids were little, they would wake on St. Patrick's Day and find magical little green leprechaun feet all over the house. Giggling with excitement, they would follow the clues to find hidden treasures. Now I just pour a green beer and kiss the first person who remotely looks Irish.

Back then, each month required festive window decals, including Easter bunnies with baskets, or marching patriots waving flags for the Fourth of July, or generic birthday balloons so the windows wouldn't be bare. After a while, I got lazy. The ceramic Halloween pumpkin worked just fine as a Thanksgiving cornucopia, and later it held a Christmas poinsettia. That silly utility pumpkin stored Valentine's candy and summer suntan lotion before it was time again for Halloween. The years seem to dull the holiday spirit, and now I usually walk past the seasonal décor aisle and head straight for the liquor department. I'll thank my lucky stars to have a Jameson's Irish whiskey to honor St. Patrick, and there will be no little green feet involved.

I continue to bring out the boxes of decorations for Christmas. I gently unwrap the thirty-year-old ornaments, hang the well-worn jingle bells, and arrange the special nativity set. Monogrammed stockings line the mantel surrounded by festive Santas and regal nutcrackers. I'm a sap for Christmas music and begin playing it on the day after Thanksgiving. I love all of it—except for the demented tune about Grandma getting run over by a reindeer. You can bet your stuffed goose that if this grandmother gets creamed by a wild animal on Christmas Eve, the family better not jump up to pick banjos and sing about it. I expect at least five hours of solemn sorrow before anyone plans a boisterous party.

Every Valentine's Day, I'm reminded of my dear friend Carol who has heart disease. We've shared decades of laughter and good times, but now she needs a pacemaker. And that breaks my heart. When we're together, I monitor her health before sharing humorous anecdotes because I don't want to stop and call the ambulance before I arrive at the punch line.

We have a running joke that is more than 25 years old. We were managers at a corporation in Boise and had worked several months to organize a seminar for business women. We volunteered our time and talents while we also worked full-time jobs and had husbands and children at home. I ended one stressful day with a joke.

"Are you always funny?" she asked.

"No," I answered. "I come in spurts."

I was exhausted and didn't mean anything risqué by the comment, but after I said it we both dissolved into tears of laughter. That line has sustained us through the years.

After age 50, the days on the calendar seem to pass faster than they did when we were younger. We just finish the last of the discounted candy that we bought the week after Valentine's Day when the snow disappears and flowers begin to wiggle out of the mud. Now is the time to pause and burst into song by singing "Sunrise, Sunset" from *Fiddler on the Roof.*

"Swiftly fly the years. One season following another, laden with happiness and tears."

That song causes me to cry like a middle-aged woman in need of chocolate and/or alcohol. Wait here while I go get some.

Okay, I'm back now and feeling much better.

Spring is my favorite season, and I'm grateful to experience another one. At my age, I've seen more than I'll see again, unless I live to be 120, and that's not likely no matter how often I floss. Springtime at midlife is bittersweet because the world is abundant with rebirth and new growth, but it also brings new aches and pains with each rain shower. And the only new growth I have is the sporadic eruption of more black hairs on my chin.

I love the renewal that comes with spring. Late for a meeting on a day in early May, I quickly drove down the driveway and then saw a vision so breathtaking that I stopped the car and stared. A spotlight of sunshine had emerged from a cluster of pastel clouds resting over the eastern mountains to shine directly onto a flowering plum tree in the front yard. As if on stage following a grand performance, the tree displayed its branches, radiant in the morning mist and completely covered with a crown of pure white flowers. I applauded with gratitude. And for the first time that spring, I noticed the vibrant azaleas were waving tender new fuchsia blossoms in a tribute to a quote by Robin Williams: "Spring is nature's way of saying, 'Let's party!'"

Rains washed away the blossoms, a reminder that the beauty of youth fades quickly. The gorgeous tree in the front yard also is nature's way of telling me that while I'm dashing around with my overloaded calendar, I'm missing the splendor that I have right here at home. That morning after I saw the sunlit tree, I cancelled my meeting, got another cup of coffee, and sat on the patio to be serenaded by happy songbirds. At least I think they were happy. I don't know bird language so they could have been arguing over who ate the last piece of worm pie or whose turn it was to de-poop the nest.

When summer finally arrives, I'm like a goofy kid on vacation. Even if the temperature is a chilly 68 degrees, I'm wearing shorts and sandals because the calendar says it's June. Dig out the grill because Studley and I are making our barbecued ribs, and I believe with all my heart and taste buds that our ribs can create world peace and bring nations together.

We prepare 10 racks of ribs for our annual Father's Day BBQ to share with an amusing assortment of family and friends. By the end of the feast, the food is gone and everyone is happy with life and at peace with the universe. The secret to profoundly excellent ribs is in my rub and steaming technique and in Studley's Texas-style sauce. The recipe is at the end of this chapter, so don't stop reading.

Summer isn't complete without a celebration on July 4th. Most cities organize a patriotic parade and fireworks, but for some true explosive entertainment we escape to the mountains to Crouch, Idaho where the local citizens organize a dangerous and horrifying experience not to be missed. The normal population is fewer than 500 full-time residents, and the entire county has only four people per square mile. But summer brings the vacationers and those with second homes. That's also when the crazies come down from the hills. And they have ammunition.

On July 4th the one street in Crouch is lined with more than 1,000 people who come with the hopes of still being alive and unbloodied after midnight. The only gas pump is turned off and guarded by police because one errant rocket could hit the gas line and ignite the entire town. At dusk, a year's salary of expensive fireworks begins in the middle of the street. Firecrackers, spinners, noise makers, sparklers, exploding stars, roman candles, and comets are a few of the pyrotechnics ignited for several hours. And, that's just from the toddlers.

All ages of people meander the streets, walking through burned out debris and lighting new whistle rockets and flares. Several people hoist huge wheels of 500 firecrackers and then pile them in the street and offer children the opportunity to light the fuses. Beer and liquor flow freely, bands perform raucous music, and grizzled old miners hop over spinning fireworks. Miraculously, no one gets hurt.

Studley and I join in the fun and by the end of the day, we have officially celebrated and make our way over the carnage to our cabin. The police continue to guard the gas pumps and smile. They say they would rather have fireworks in town instead of out in the woods because the possibility of burning down the restaurant and grocery store is a preferable alternative to starting a forest fire.

The fifth of July in Crouch is quiet, except for the occasional gunshot and leftover duds that suddenly explode and cause some horses to stampede through town. We invite guests to join us for the annual event, but they must bring an insurance waiver.

The best part of late summer is the promise of fresh tomatoes. Not the hard, flavorless balls in the grocery stores but luscious ripened tomatoes from local gardens. I'm happy to the point of exhilaration with a plate of sliced tomatoes, mozzarella cheese, and fresh basil drizzled with imported olive oil. And red wine. Don't forget the wine.

September is a treat for the senses. The air feels fresher, the colors of nature burst with vibrancy, and morning coffee tastes better on a cool patio as geese squawk overhead—the original snowbirds heading south for the winter. And for me, September always brings the faint smell of early harvest: the raw-earth odor of dirt-coated potatoes conveying into damp cellars, fresh-baked apple pies cooling on Grandma's flour sack tea towels, and the delightful aroma of a young Beaujolais—new wine that is bottled right after fermentation without aging.

In September, our family celebrates three birthdays, two wedding anniversaries, and a grandchild's birthday. For my September birthday, I search for a nice Beaujolais because there is no time to waste. After several decades of abundant living, I'm hesitant to wait too much longer for wine to mature. I resemble a kid in a candy store at closing time—too many wonderful choices, so little time.

As part of a wonderful cultural and universal tradition, I recently folded baby clothes with my pregnant daughter-in-law. "Oh, look at this one!" we exclaimed with each tiny onesie. I took extra time to fold the sleeper that my son once wore.

Our family celebrated another milestone this week as my daughter's daughter started kindergarten. She wore shoes that light up with every step. I want shoes like that. I also want to experience the freshness of a new adventure, new friends, and new ideas to learn. In the autumn of life, there is still so much to do, and I don't want to miss anything. Well, if I had to do it all over again, I would like to avoid all those painful trips to the principal's office.

Fall brings the excitement and terror of the holidays. It's normal to feel guilty because your Thanksgiving experience never resembles the Norman Rockwell painting of a happy family gathered around a lovely table as Grandma in her white apron proudly delivers a perfect turkey. Instead, the family feast often includes a drunk uncle, at least one pouting teenager, Grandpa blowing his nose on the fine linen, a power outage, gag-inducing gravy, cousins chasing each other with the electric carving knife, a devil-nephew cramming olive pits up his nose, and a quarrel between some adults who should be sitting at the children's table. Maybe it's time to put down the drumsticks and the shotguns and just relax. If you get to midnight on Thanksgiving without a single drama, count your blessings, indeed.

The holiday season brings added stress for blended families, but we've discovered how to survive without a food fight, bloodletting, or lawsuits. Our family tree could be in danger of falling over because the branches are laden with sporadic offshoots, new in-laws, old stepparents, and assorted children who share multiple homes. But because of extra care, these roots are strong, and our tree can hold the chaotic collection of yours, mine, ours, various ex-spouses, and a few confused grandparents.

During the holiday season, we welcome everyone into the family, and for a splendid moment before someone falls into the Christmas tree or a kid rips off the head of a cousin's new Barbie, there will be peace in the valley.

Blended families add chaos to the holidays, and planning a stress-free schedule requires maximum organizational skills, saintly tolerance, nimble flexibility, and extra mugs of fortified eggnog. Even if the holidays are months away, you should plan now for the possible scenarios.

You could be standing in the buffet line next to your ex-spouse, your stepson may demand to bring his mother and her new boyfriend to your home for brunch, or your son's stepdaughters might want to stay at their father's place because you don't have cable television.

It's all fun and games until Grandma throws down her cane and demands to know who all the people are coming and going.

To prepare for the festivities and retain a tiny bit of sanity, start planning the holiday schedule months in advance. The best situations involve divorced parents who can cooperate and negotiate holiday schedules as they decide custody issues involving their children. We all know mean-spirited, immature parents who refuse to budge, and that only hurts their children. These parents should receive nothing but coal in their stockings, and they better start saving money for their kids' future counseling sessions.

Our blended family resembles a crock pot of beef soup mixed with sugar and spice with a side of jambalaya and a touch of hot sauce spread over four generations.

My husband and I each have two adult children. My daughter married a man who already had a daughter, and then they had two more daughters. My son married a woman with two girls, and they had another baby. My ex-husband lives in the area and is included in family birthdays and other events. Somehow it all works, and no one has threatened anyone with a weapon, so far.

There are fourteen Christmas stockings hanging over the mantel, and we'll need to build another one if any more members join the family. I'm uncomfortable with the label "step-grandchild" so I'll just call all of them my grandkids. They don't mind, and some of those lucky kids have four sets of doting grandparents. Score!

Here are three final suggestions for surviving the holidays with a blended family: First, have a sense of humor because it's better to laugh at the commotion instead of breaking something. Second, take plenty of photographs to identify everyone because Grandma is still baffled. Third, make time to appreciate the creative collection of characters in your unique family, believing that each one adds a definite spice. In the spirit of the holidays, choose to make it work.

Sometimes the best plans get burned along with the roast. It's tempting to go over the river and through the woods and then keep on going just to avoid all the glossy images, trite platitudes, and impossible expectations about the holidays. Forget Rockwell's famous portrait because most grandmothers don't wear white aprons after fixing a messy meal, and there's a good chance that this year they'll introduce their new boyfriends instead of picture-perfect platters of browned Butterballs. And Martha Stewart is not coming over, so forget the hand-painted placemats and pilgrim-shaped gelatin molds.

After a few decades, we older women ease up on the stressful requirements and have no qualms about using prepared gravy mixes, boxed stuffing, and leftover Halloween napkins. As long as the turkey is done and the wine is open, we're just fine. My mother's generation washed Thanksgiving dishes until their hands turned numb while the menfolk watched TV, smoked, and farted. My daughter's generation finds both men and women working together in the kitchen. But after about five minutes, the men are instructed to get the hell out of the kitchen. Sometimes tradition works better.

After experiencing more than fifty Thanksgivings, most of us have at least one that came at a pivotal time in our lives. For me, Thanksgiving provided a poignant perspective a few years ago when I was a middle-aged divorcee and it seemed that everyone in the entire world was part of a happy, loving, and thankful couple. I survived the holiday for two reasons: I never miss a good meal, and I was determined to show gratitude. The second reason was more challenging than the first. I tackled the dilemma by doing something completely spontaneous and crazy: that Thanksgiving, I booked a reservation for a cruise the following March to Costa Rica, Panama, and Cozumel.

The cruise was called, ironically, the Gratitude Cruise. I found the information while researching one of my favorite speakers, Dr. Sue Morter. I had attended her International Living Seminar as part of a business conference. She's a healer and a teacher, and she focuses on the connections between the mind, the body, and the spirit. I know this sounds way too New Age for my old-age sensibilities, but when you hit bottom, you look for the light, any light.

Being alone on a cruise can make for some interesting experiences. I sat at different dining tables and chatted with strangers every night. Some were suspicious of my intentions while others felt pity that I had no friends. I assured them I wasn't a total loser nor a felon on the run. A flashy, obnoxious guy named Stephano offered to escort me back to my cabin until I informed him about my terrible, contagious disease and that my invalid aunt was quarantined in the room. When he offered to take me dancing, I yielded to my deepest Darth Vader voice and said, "There is no escape. Don't make me destroy you." He moved on to the next table.

During the week, the programs included music and workshops about inner peace, meditation, acceptance, resilience, and, most important, gratitude. After wallowing in the negative emotions associated with my divorce, the messages were the antidote to the poison that consumed my thoughts. I returned renewed, refreshed, and ready to live out loud with an attitude of gratitude. But I refused to buy the bongo drums, chant lyrics, or incense burners. Remember, I live in Idaho.

After the cruise, I participated in the holiday and year-end activities. One evening I hunkered down in my flannel jammies with some peppermint schnapps and wrote in my journal. I summarized all the fun and fabulous, the rotten and wretched, and the clever and comedic parts of the year. I've written in a personal journal every December for the past thirty-five years. I began writing soon after the invention of electricity but just before the advent of the personal computer. My earlier entries written with a pen are more personal than the electronic version, but now I'm hooked on word processing, so I print my yearly musings and insert them into my journal. Besides, I can never find a pen that works.

Before I write, I shuffle through the past years to find poignant reminders that life has kicked me in the gut a few times, but the splendid days far outnumber the crappy ones. My goal is for that trend to continue.

I laugh when I read about how miserable I was about my weight after the birth of my second baby more than thirty years ago. I would LOVE to weigh that now! It's touching to reread details about my children's first words, their growth charts, and their early bowel movements…things only a mother could document.

My journals also tell the story of essential parts of my life that have been damaged, lost, and reclaimed: love, family, jobs, homes, health, and money. I've made huge mistakes in real estate and financial investments, mostly because I relied upon the advice of (former) friends, but I've claimed success because of the strong relationships with my husband and children and with satisfying achievements in my career. Now I know what matters, and it's not the volatile dividends of my once-glorious but currently worthless NASDAQ stocks.

My collected journals hold items that symbolize special occasions: a pressed flower, a published poem, old photos, theatre tickets, and an assortment of favorite wine labels. The journals are stored in a safe place so they won't be thrown out when my office is featured on an episode of *Hoarders*.

The journals also contain a few of my favorite recipes. My grown children anticipate certain holiday dishes from

their childhood, and they throw fits if they come for di
and I have changed the recipes.

One of my family's favorite recipes is pecan pie with
real whipped cream. I used to buy frozen whipped topping
for my pies until I read the label and discovered that the
product contains enough chemical ingredients to make
my internal organs explode. I come with labels that could
include left-handed, menopausal, witty, Presbyterian. Any
one of my identities could offend someone, but I'm still less
toxic than Cool Whip.

It's important for food to be labeled because I should
know if the product I'm buying to feed my family contains
Polysorbate 60—a chemically-derived emulsifier in Cool
Whip that has been linked to organ toxicity, diarrhea, and
tumors in laboratory rats. The label also informs me that
this fluffy, sweet concoction that looks so appealing in a
Jell-O parfait also has synthetic wax, hydrogenated oils, and
high fructose corn syrup. I should just eat poison instead.

Here are a few of our traditional recipes:

World Peace BBQ Ribs

Place a few racks of pork baby back ribs on a rack over a
broiler pan.

Create a rub of grated lemon rind, grated fresh ginger,
and lots of pressed fresh garlic. Pat the paste on the ribs.
(Save the lemons for iced tea or water.)

Pour boiling water into the bottom of the pan and cover
with a tent of tin foil. Bake for an hour at 350 degrees.
Open a bottle of wine and test for flavor. Test again.

For the sauce, Studley starts with a bottle of hickory-smoked BBQ sauce and one flat beer in a sauce pan. (To make beer flat, leave a bottle open for several hours or heat it 20 seconds in the microwave.) Add two cubes of butter (yes, he is a true Southerner), some Montreal Steak Seasoning, and some garlic salt. Simmer for about 40 minutes. (This sauce would make horse manure tasty.) While it simmers, share some beer and/or wine with your spouse. Then throw the steamed ribs on the BBQ, slather with plenty of sauce, and wait about 10 minutes for the magic to happen. Share more beer and wine with guests.

Serve with salads, fruit, veggies, rolls and more butter, and lots of paper towels. These ribs pair nicely with cold Miller Lite Beer and several bottles of bold cabernet. End the meal with some pie and brownies. Then sit around, rub your full bellies, and offer toasts to those who have a father. Typically, that would include everyone.

Meatball Bar

It's like a salad bar but with lots of calories.

Mix together a pound of lean ground beef, a pound of spicy Italian bulk sausage, three eggs, one heaping cup grated fresh Parmesan cheese, about one cup bread crumbs with Italian spices, chopped fresh parsley, and salt and pepper. Shape into balls and cook on cookie sheets at 325 degrees for about 30 minutes. Serve with a variety of sauces, including barbecue, sweet and sour, marinara, and cream. Add assorted salads and it's a party.

Mama Lainey's Potato Soup

Brown one pound Italian sausage and one pound spicy Italian sausage. Near the end, toss in ½ cup each of diced onions, green peppers, celery, and some minced fresh garlic. Peel and boil six Idaho russet potatoes in a pot of water 15 minutes with two tablespoons of mustard seed. Remove half the water, add the meat mixture, add two cups of cream, and heat but don't boil. Add salt and pepper to taste. Making this soup is the easiest way to become a family hero.

Christmas Prime Rib

Order a 6-pound standing rib roast, cut and tied. Let stand to room temperature on a rack in a roasting pan. Make a paste of beef broth, garlic salt, coarsely ground black pepper, and curry powder. Smear it over the roast, including the sides and end. Insert meat thermometer and roast for 20 minutes at 500 degrees. Then turn down the oven to 350 degrees, but don't open the door for two more hours. Check for doneness and adjust accordingly. Serve with horseradish and poppy seed potatoes.

Poppy Seed Potatoes

Peel and cube six large Idaho potatoes, cover with water in a pot, and boil for 10 minutes. Drain. Combine one heaping cup grated sharp cheddar cheese, one pint sour cream, ½ cup light cream, 1/8 cup poppy seeds, four chopped green onions. Add the cooked spuds and pour into a casserole dish. Bake covered at 350 degrees for 20 minutes, uncover and bake 10 more minutes.

Baked Won Ton Appetizer

Find a package of won ton wrappers in the produce section. Slice them in half. Melt ½ cube of butter in a cookie sheet with edges. Lay won ton strips in the melted butter, turn over so both sides are buttered. Sprinkle with ½ cup grated fresh Parmesan cheese or with sugar and cinnamon. Bake on low heat, about 300 degrees, until brown. Cool on paper towels. Guests love these.

∼

Desperately Seeking Self-Confidence

At my age, getting out of bed each morning should be an Olympic event worthy of a gold medal. I can hear the breathless announcers:

"She's got one foot out, Bob. Will she be able to move the other one in the next five minutes?"

"Look, Brian. Now both feet are on the floor. The form is a bit wobbly, but she stuck the landing!"

The crowd goes wild. I hobble to the podium in my well-worn nightgown, my hair is disheveled, and I squint without my glasses. I bend to receive the medal, but I need help getting up again. My back aches, my neck is stiff, and one leg has a cramp, but I'm still standing. A single tear rolls from my eye but catches in a wrinkle. Yes, I did it! Now, what's for breakfast?

I've enjoyed watching the Olympics and am amazed at the physical and mental strength of the athletes. I wish I had a fraction of their discipline. And as the late comedian George Burns once said, "If I knew I would live this long, I would have taken better care of myself."

If you are what you eat, I'm a gigantic chocolate chip cookie floating in a vat of red wine. Two years ago, I boldly announced that I had a new zeal to live long enough to irritate my future great-grandchildren. I enrolled in an intense exercise program with the goal of jogging a 5K race in the St. Luke's Women's Fitness Celebration. I knew there was a fifty-fifty chance I would make it to the starting line and then take a detour to the scone booth. By the time I finished, most of the crowd was gone, so only a few spectators remained to cheer me to the finish line. But I was one of the few joggers to have grandchildren waiting at the end. I felt as if I had completed a major marathon, so of course I celebrated with chocolate chip cookies and wine.

The fitness program included workout sessions, meditation, goal-setting exercises, calorie tracking, and menu planning. The instructor met us at a grocery store and taught us to shop on the outside of the aisles—that's where the fresh, organic produce, dairy products, and lean meats are displayed. Now I'm afraid to go near the rows of packaged, processed foods because some bell will ring, lights will flash, and I'll be disqualified from class.

It's still amazing to return from the store with kale and cucumbers instead of cake and candy. I'm trying to cook and eat healthier, and I even made a dinner with quinoa—an organic, high-protein grain—sautéed with fresh vegetables and herbs. Studley added a cube of butter, some Cajun spice, and a pork chop and said it was delicious. In the true test of discipline, I've limited the amount of red wine that I enjoy. Note the word "limited" as opposed to "eliminated." Not even world-class athletes are perfect in everything!

I can attribute my unhealthy physique and eating habits to my genes—we've got several obese family members in the clan—and to the fact that I love to eat and drink. The first time I lost weight rapidly was when I gave birth to another human. But I only did that twice and that was sufficient. The second time was when I had my wisdom teeth pulled. A diet of water and gelatin resulted in a dramatic loss of twelve pounds in just a week. I was considering having more teeth pulled, but then the weight returned with a few extra pounds for good measure.

My mother's idea of creative cooking was to heat together two different cans of Campbell's soup—such as Chicken Noodle and Beef Barley—and then top it with a cup of oyster crackers. Voila! A gourmet meal down on the farm! With respect for my mom, she also could prepare an evening banquet of two dozen fried pork chops, a mixing bowl of mashed potatoes, a vat of green beans with bacon, a platter of buttered corn on the cob, and a pan of warm apple cobbler with ice cream. Anticipating what would appear on the family table became a guessing game of feast or famine, which helps explain my lifelong battle with weight.

Over the decades, I've gained and lost the weight of a Buick. Or two, depending upon the make and model. Every few years, I try the latest fad—lost a ton with Atkins and gained it all back in four hours, joined Weight Watchers and developed anxiety attacks because of the weigh-ins, attempted Zumba and broke my foot just before my son's wedding, and I even tried using smaller plates, but those salad plates still can hold six brownies. Sigh.

When I reached middle age, I finally acknowledged that I like to eat and probably would do so for the rest of my life. So I decided to learn how to cook. A few years ago, I attended a week-long cooking school in Tuscany, Italy, the ultimate place for good eating (and drinking, but that's another story). There I learned how to make delicious sauces, exquisite pasta dishes, and chicken parmesan so magnificent that it becomes a religious experience. Italians know how to cook—and eat. The *mangiar bene*—good meal—takes all day to prepare but is worth its weight in wine bottles. And those wonderful Italians keep healthy because they walk everywhere, don't sit around watching TV, and enjoy the sex lives of rabbits in heat.

I only fix a big meal a few times a month, and the rest of the time Studley and I try to eat small, healthy meals. Last night, I tried a "faux" Italian meal of lean turkey and spinach meatballs with whole wheat pasta. Let's just say that Studley choked down the meal and then said, lovingly of course, "I don't like dry balls." And, no, he shouldn't.

I admit that the meal was a disaster, but here is the dilemma: I lost a pound. So, maybe it's okay to ruin a fine Italian meal once in a while for the sake of the main goal—I want to lose enough weight so I can prepare a gourmet meal and truly enjoy it. And there won't be any soup cans involved. *Buon appetito!*

Besides the "weight issue," I also have a "clutter problem." The main areas of my house are showplace ready, but my office and garage offer proof of chaos and confusion. I've been called a Pandemonium Packrat, and that is not the name of a rock and roll band.

I have a dreaded fear that Oprah's camera crew will burst into my house any day and start filming for a television show about pitiful packrats who should be institutionalized.

They'll find my box of 4-H ribbons from 1962. It's packed along with my blue sweater from the 1969 Wendell Pep Band. (I played saxophone.) Then they'll find my dad's army jacket and my grandmother's hat. They're right beside the box of single forty-five records, featuring Sam the Sham singing "Lil' Red Riding Hood," and Herman's Hermits crooning "Silhouettes," and Gerry and the Pacemakers swooning "Ferry across the Mersey."

I know I can buy and download a digitally enhanced version of those old songs, but I can't bear to part with the scratchy-sounding music from my memories.

A few years ago, I threw out 200 garbage bags of former-treasures-turned-junk. I was moving and had to clean out the basement. Some of the special items I found included my children's baby teeth—in little packets with labels and diagrams of their mouths. I had carefully sketched the location of each tooth and when it was removed as if *my* children's teeth were the most spectacular treasures in all the world. Subsequently, I discovered that other children also lost their teeth but instead of becoming collected heirlooms the teeth were rewarded a dollar each by the Tooth Fairy. I guess I owe money, with interest, to my children.

I also found a petrified turtle's egg that I've had for over twenty years. No, I don't know why I kept it, but it was unique and no one else had one. When I spied it at the bottom of a dusty drawer I squealed with delight and rushed to show my neighbor. She wasn't impressed. But she asked if she could have my broken guitar that I used 30 years ago as a camp counselor. I agreed, as long as she took the egg. It was a deal.

And, so very bittersweet, I found a small bottle of breast milk tucked in the back of the freezer. My youngest is twenty-seven. He doesn't need it anymore. I had moved that bottle from house to house over the years, never wanting to part with the last essential connection to my baby. Some of those who breastfed their babies will understand, while others will suggest counseling. I couldn't throw away the milk because I worked too hard for it. So I wrapped it in tissue paper, tucked it into a Crown Royal velvet pouch, and buried it under the rose bush in the back yard. The home's new owners may redo the garden someday and discover the strange burial site. I hope they don't contact the police.

My packrat affliction does give me a few moments of vindication. Once my son, my daughter and her husband, and their baby girl came over for dinner. They stayed longer than expected, and the ten-month-old baby was getting sleepy, but they hadn't brought pajamas. "I have some!" I exclaimed, with glee. I had saved and washed several pairs of my children's pajamas for my new granddaughter. Soon she was wearing the cute outfit that my son wore twenty-six years ago.

Seeing her in the old jammies made me happy. My children then gently suggested that I could donate the rest of their old clothes to charity, and I agreed. But I'm still keeping the boxes of their papers from elementary school. You never know when suddenly those papers will become valuable collector's items!

Another cobweb-encrusted item I found on the top shelf in the garage was the cheap version of a Stairmaster machine. It was only two footpads hooked to strong springs, but the advertisement guaranteed that regular use of the contraption would tone legs, firm the buttocks, melt away unwanted pounds, and cause the user to sing and dance like

Julie Andrews on a mountaintop in *The Sound of Music*. To my shock and dismay, none of those claims were true. So it was tossed into the donation pile to be unused by another hapless dreamer with a sagging butt.

When I was a little girl, meaning a long, long time ago, I witnessed my mother's morning ritual of stepping onto a machine in her bedroom, securing a strap around her waist, and then flipping a switch that made her entire body shake like mud in a blender. Since then, I have suppressed these horrifying memories by consuming large bowls of peanut M&Ms and cases of red wine and by avoiding blenders. Even the noise of a fancy margarita machine can throw me into a catatonic panic attack that only can be soothed by at least two of the tasty frozen concoctions.

My mother's diets were legendary. Once she tried magic pills that made her lose weight so fast she looked awful. We found out years later the doctor with the secret prescription was selling narcotics. So my mother joined a national weight loss program. One evening the entire membership of the local diet group came to our house for an evening meeting. I watched in amazement as each one removed jewelry, shoes, and extra clothing before stepping on the scale. Excuses for the inevitable weight gain ranged from chronic constipation to the time of the month. I had no idea what they were talking about. I just stayed around because they always served some decadent dessert after the weigh-in.

Fast forward fifty years, and I am the card-carrying member of the "Tried and Failed Every Diet on the Planet" club. To quote the late, great Erma Bombeck, "I keep trying to go on a diet, and I've tried going to the gym. I've exercised with women so thin that buzzards followed them to their cars. And, in two decades, I've lost a total of 789 pounds. I should be hanging from a charm bracelet."

In my spare time, that blessed moment between 1:00 and 2:00 p.m., I enjoy watching documentaries on Netflix because it's easier to justify than watching soft porn. Lately, I've been hooked on food films. Now I'm scared to death about all the crap in our food. I grew up on a farm, and we ate our crops and our livestock (except for the horses).

The last documentary I watched was *Fat, Sick and Nearly Dead* by Joe Cross. The show advocates the use of juicers, and it shows how obese, unhealthy people gave up chewing and became healthy, happy, productive members of society by drinking juice. For every meal. I immediately put down my box of Girl Scout cookies, mainly because it was empty, and vowed to try this plan. My friend was on the juice diet, and she looked great. (Of course, she was born beautiful, but that's not the point.)

I had a $100 rebate from purchasing a pair of contacts. I took that with my 20-percent-off coupon to Bed, Bath & Beyond and ordered a Breville Juice Fountain Plus. With my rebate and coupon, it only cost $30. It arrived by mail the following week, so I stocked up on red beets, celery, apples, cucumbers, spinach, ginger root, lemons, and peppers. It was great fun to watch whole apples and beets instantly whirl into juice, and I imagined myself as a mad but merry scientists concocting powerful potions and enchanting elixirs. (I really need to get out more.)

Then I reached for a juice glass but changed my mind. In an erroneous attempt to fool myself, I poured the beet mixture into a wine glass. I swirled the glass to note the legs. They were thick. Then I sniffed the aroma to test the nose.

That brought back memories of my grandmother's dank underground cellar. Finally, I sipped with refined expertise. Remember how we used to fool our babies by pretending the blob of baby food was on an airplane heading into their mouths? That didn't work then, either. I regret corrupting my best wine glass.

After a few days, I was running a small juice factory and also running down the hall to the bathroom. I didn't dare leave the house. I already knew the location of every public bathroom within a fifty-mile radius from my home, but that wasn't good enough. I thought about pulling a Porta-Potty on a trailer behind my car, but they don't deliver, and I knew I couldn't make it to their store. So, I eased up a little on the amount and frequency. Now I only have juice once or twice a day. That leaves plenty of time to consume my other favorite juice. It's made from fermented grapes.

Being embarrassed in public is a common occurrence. I often experience profound humiliation with a daunting magnitude that would send most people screaming into the forest, never to return. After all these years, I accept the fact that I probably will trip and fall in a busy crosswalk, fart during a massage, drop my passport into a foreign toilet, or sprout broccoli in my teeth while giving a motivational speech. However, I still cringe at the memory of a recent embarrassment.

Due to stress, deadlines, and too much caffeine, I had attacked my fingernails like a crazed wolverine, leaving bloody stumps that were too painful to use even to shampoo my hair. Of course, this was on a day when I had a Very Important Meeting with some Very Important People at a Very Private Club in Boise. Not even my best St. Johns knit suit could hide my tortured hands. It was time to leave, so I frantically pawed through my drawers looking for some fake nails to glue onto my fingers but only found some press-on toenails. The instructions on the box guaranteed that I didn't need glue because the adhesive would last for a week. I slapped those gleaming toenails onto the ends of my ravaged fingers, picked up my briefcase, and dashed to the meeting, feeling smug that I had successfully survived yet another personal crisis.

At the Very Exclusive Club, I was escorted to the premium table and introduced to a sophisticated woman who looked like a model in a Ralph Lauren ad and a man who appeared to possess all the knowledge of the universe. As she shook my right hand, the toenail on my right thumb suddenly popped off and landed on the white linen tablecloth. I mumbled something about "that darned broken nail" and plucked it from the table. After exchanging professional pleasantries, we ordered herb-infused tomato bisque. As I took a sip, the toenail on the left hand snapped off and plopped into the soup. I tried to push it down with my spoon, but it kept bobbing up as if pleading to be rescued. Apparently, toes are wider and flatter than fingernails, and these things wouldn't last the hour let alone a week. I resisted the temptation to say, "Waiter, there's a toenail in my soup."

My table companions cleared their throats and started their conversation about how I should diversify my investment portfolio to take advantage of opportunities in emerging markets. As they talked, I held my hands in my lap, working quickly to pry off the remaining nails so they wouldn't sporadically shoot from my hand and put out someone's eye. Two of the stubborn nails validated the claim on the box and wouldn't release until I ripped them off and the wounded fingers started to bleed again. I discretely wrapped the linen napkin around my hand until it looked like one of those bandaged fists from a war movie. By the time the elegant woman was displaying a chart of recommended international equity funds, I was sitting on a pile of discarded toenails, applying white-linen pressure to my hemorrhaging fingertips, and pretending everything was okay.

I want the dignified waiter at The Arid Club to know that I really regret leaving that mess. But maybe he overheard some good hints about investing and will remove my name from the list of "Guests to Never Allow Back Inside."

As long as I'm confessing incidents that include acts of egregious humiliation and/or pathetic ineptitude, I might as well include my Rules of Life, which correctly include the admonishment to avoid laxatives before participating in strenuous outdoor activities.

I've never been one to follow rules. A long list of frustrated teachers, exasperated parents, and humorless police officers can confirm that fact. It's not that I'm overly rebellious; it's just that I prefer to have my own way. About everything. This attitude can be annoying to others.

However, after living this long, I do adhere to a few Rules of Life:

- Never assume people will appreciate that you are alive. (This fact comes in handy when dealing with sales clerks, bank tellers, neighbors, classmates, audiences, exspouses, etc.)

- Always tip waiters, hairdressers, and physical therapists. (Acknowledge that these people help you eat, look better, and feel great. They deserve a tip for dealing with you.)

- Don't timidly giggle when you can guffaw. (Laugh until your belly aches, your eyes water, and some kind of liquid spurts out your nose. You'll look stupid but it feels so good!)

- Avoid laxatives before playing in a golf tournament.

I just added that last rule. For those of us past a certain age, IBS does not mean the International Banking System. No, we're blessed with a malady known as Irritable Bowel Syndrome (sorry if you're having breakfast). We never know when or where our bodies will decide to perform necessary bodily functions. I've always admired those who have been in the military because they get up, grab the newspaper, and go to the bathroom. Every day. However, many middle-aged women greet a BM like those winners in the Publishers Clearing House Sweepstakes ads. We're so overjoyed that we want someone to deliver balloons and a big check.

I recently played in a golf tournament. A few days before the tournament, I was so miserable that I downed several "gentle softeners" to assist Mother Nature. Well, she was out of town and didn't return the call…until I stepped up to the first tee box. I know some of you are nodding your heads. Yes, that's when the gurgling started.

Golf courses are designed by men, probably with military experience, who have already done their daily duty and don't need restrooms. When I golf, I calculate how long it will take to get to the lonely restroom at the far end of the course, and I have been known to jump into the cart and take off over the next fairway. Others golfers do not appreciate this, but many of the "seasoned" women raise their clubs in silent salute.

Anyway, at a recent tournament I made a frantic decision to break the rules (golf has too many rules, anyway). It was Studley's turn to hit when I felt the dreaded gurgle of doom and knew I had only a few minutes to get to the restroom or be forever banned from the private golf club. I threw Studley his fairway club and putter and took off in the cart.

"Where are you going?" he called after me.

"To save my pride and my white shorts," I hollered as I bumped the cart through the rough terrain. The ride didn't help my situation and I was desperate by the time I got to the facility. The women's restroom was occupied so I dashed into the men's restroom. There are times when you just don't deal with proper etiquette and protocol. At that moment, the men's restroom was my port in the storm, and I was relieved in many ways. I returned by the second hole, refreshed and rewarded, and hit the longest drive of my life. Studley and the rest of my scramble partners now want me to repeat the lucky technique for the next tournament.

~

Blended Families — A Bit Shaken and Stirred

Unless your mother-in-law is a convicted felon or a pole dancer at the Kit Kat Klub, you should spend quality one-on-one time with her. After all, she raised the person you married. If she lives far away, keep in contact with letters, phone calls, and photos of the kids. Encourage her to use the Internet to share messages and videos. And if she continually repeats the same stories over and over, just nod politely. Then you won't feel so guilty at her funeral.

Most young, married women juggle a three-page to-do list, and visiting with the mother-in-law probably isn't a top priority. As I recall, that goal wasn't included in my Top 100 Action Items as I managed a hectic schedule that included active children, a full-time job, a cluttered house, and a husband who preferred to eat dinner before midnight. Now, after all these years, I regret not spending more time with my mothers-in-law. (Yes, I had more than one.)

We never lived in the same state, so I didn't really know them before they passed away. The most time I spent with one was when I sang "Ave Maria" at her funeral Mass. (I love singing in Latin because no one knows if I mess up the words. If I forget a phrase, I just substitute "Ave" several times and add a wordless aria.) I sang out of respect because she was a good person. I would rather have shared pie and wine with her while she was still alive.

I recently had the pleasure of being with my son-in-law for a beer and a few days later with my daughter-in-law for leftover Thanksgiving pecan pie and wine. I highly recommend both activities. My son-in-law loves my daughter, is devoted to their daughters, and works hard at his job. Those facts are like music to the feeble ears of any mother-in-law. My daughter-in-law has the same positive qualities, and she is a lovely young woman. They provide a healthy, nurturing home for their children, and they include me in activities. I never want to deserve the comment, "Oh crap, do we have to invite your mother?"

Some of my friends have estranged relationships with their in-laws, and the annual Thanksgiving feast often turns awkward if the seating arrangements are not compatible with the guests. I've solved that problem because the food at my house is served buffet style, first-come-first-served, and then find your own chair if you can. One exception: Great-Grandma gets to go first because she's in a wheelchair. That's one advantage of being the oldest.

The decades quickly tumble past, and a young woman soon becomes an older woman who becomes a mother-in-law. I want to become the type of mother-in-law that won't be poisoned, abandoned, or sent away to a nice home in a foreign country. I'll try to be someone who gives advice when asked and doesn't gloat that my turkey stuffing is still my child's favorite. We mothers just want our darling adult children to be happy, and that means we know they are in loving, supportive marriages. And if my son-in-law or daughter-in-law wants some advice, I'll eagerly meet them for conversation, beer, and/or pie.

Sometimes blending the family frappe takes extraordinary skills. Organizing an event with blended families requires the logistical coordination of air traffic controllers with the precision of a computerized dispatcher and the help of a licensed counselor. Uniting yours, mine, ours, and theirs becomes a calculated strategy that turns dates on the calendar into targets for negotiation. There's a reason we never saw the ex-families on the television show *The Brady Bunch*.

I grew up in a small community during a time when couples married, had children, and stayed married until they died. Some didn't speak to each other during the last twenty years of marriage, but by golly, they stayed together. Some of us guessed they were just too tired to split the sheets. And, they both loved the dog.

Our family gatherings often included more than thirty people—and none were divorced. There was minimal tactical planning required to schedule an event. Times have changed, and sometimes I feel the pressure to make sure everyone is happy. I need to get over that. Our social functions often include an eclectic combination of current and ex family members. At my stepson's high school graduation, I sat next to his mother. At my daughter's wedding, her father and I both walked her down the aisle, even though we were divorced. We do it for our children. Even the receiving line was fun because our daughter's happiness was most important.

I admire those parents who negotiate joint custody arrangements using common sense. Holiday and birthday parties are less stressful if the parents coordinate plans and speak without assaulting each other. And what child wouldn't want to be spoiled and adored by eight different grandparents?

All of my grandchildren are girls, and that's just fine because girls are fun. They want to play dress up, make crafts, sing silly songs, put glitter stars on their cheeks, and lie in the grass to watch the clouds. Boys just want to eat and break something.

Because of these girls, I'm mindful of the temptations that are waiting to capture their minds and souls. I've altered the words of a popular country song so I can sing, "Mama, don't let your babies grow up to be call girls." And I mean it.

The world's oldest profession comes with nasty consequences, so why are mothers allowing their young daughters to look like hookers? Julia Roberts glamorized prostitution in the movie *Pretty Woman,* but reality proves that it's not the best career choice. Call girls have a higher probability of becoming diseased, abused, and dead instead of being saved and supported by a handsome millionaire.

Many of us more mature women regularly fight the urge to rush over with a protective tarp when we see a group of fifth-grade girls strutting through the mall. By their clothes and makeup, they appear to be taking a break from their pole dancing gig and sauntering to hang out on the street corner. All they lack are dollar bills hanging from their belts and portable credit card readers attached to their bling-encrusted cell phones. And this is before they've had their first period.

I love to take my older granddaughters shopping for school clothes. We start with a budget and scamper through the ranks of clothes. We have some ground rules: no white pants, no high heels, and nothing with a provocative word across the rear. Fortunately, the girls are comfortable in jeans, t-shirts, tennis shoes, and hoodies. Occasionally, there will be a minor mutiny.

"Tutu, please, please can I have this?" one bright-eyed granddaughter said while holding an elaborate chiffon dress with sequins across the top.

"I don't know how that would survive the playground," I retort. "Here, look at this cute jean jacket." The one with the credit card gets to create the distraction.

A recent national study revealed that 30 percent of young girls' clothing is sexualized at fifteen major retailers. Companies spend $12 billion a year to convince little girls that they should look like tarts and tramps. A French company recently introduced a line of bras for ages four to twelve, and many stores offer padded bikinis for ten-year-olds. Over 70 percent of the clothes marketed by Abercrombie Kids feature sexy characters, provocative writing, a minimal amount of material, and designs to emphasize a girl's chest and butt. The mothers who buy these clothes soon will have a new name: Grandmother.

According to the American Academy of Pediatrics, almost 37 percent of fourteen-year-olds have had sex. Promiscuous sexual experimentation has increased, resulting in about three million cases of sexually transmitted diseases every year among teens, and there are approximately one million unwanted teenage pregnancies. Yet another study indicates that young girls have alarming afflictions with eating disorders and negative self-perceptions. I don't need to read any more studies. It's obvious that our young girls are clamoring for the type of approval that will never come from texting a naked photo that remains on the Internet forever.

I'm not a prude—I coauthored and published a book of romantic poetry titled *Daily Erotica,* but the poems are for adults. I think sexual passion is fabulous, and I can maneuver into a skimpy negligee if the lights are low and my husband promises jewelry. But when it comes to sexy six-year-olds, I agree with Dana Carvey's Church Lady. It's not pru-dent.

My grown children already have established rules as their daughters approach their pre-teen years. They won't buy clothes that turn the girls into sex objects. The parents intend to know the passwords to every social media site and watch for pedophiles or bullies. They will know their friends, establish guidelines and expectations, and lead by example. They won't allow movies, magazines, and music that glorify rape, promote promiscuous sex, and degenerate women. If their daughters complain, they will be invited to get a job and pay for room, board, computer, and Internet access. If one still throws a fit for trampy fashion, she will be assigned to write a report about "Successful Whores I Admire."

Children and grandchildren grow up fast enough, so I want to focus on fun family time while I still can skip beside them without pausing for an inhaler or a taxi. We'll encourage sports, musical instruments, dance, and art. We'll take walks together, plan vacations, play outside, and make family meals together. We'll discuss sex without blushing (but I may hold off on having them read the first few chapters of this book). The best advice I give to my grown children is to pick their battles and compromise: the short skirt is okay with leggings. (Duct tape them on, if necessary.)

Finally, analyze parental self-talk. Children and grandchildren notice if their adult role model is always critical of her or his body. They also observe healthy, loving relationships that they want to emulate. Teach them that bodies are beautiful at any age, and sex is natural and wonderful at a mature level that doesn't require Hello Kitty lip gloss. Acknowledge that a ten-year-old doesn't need a matching lace panty and bra set. Apply the money to a college fund so she can create her own business that encourages and celebrates smart women.

When first-time grandparents and step-grandparents ask me for advice on what to do with their new progeny, especially if the step-children are older than babies, I suggest to plan a play date. Not with other children, but with them. Imagine activities that don't involve money or electronics.(If that idea makes you panic, you know that it's past time for you to plan your own play day. You owe it to yourself to grab a few hours of uninterrupted, stress-free time to do whatever you want and be completely free. Making mud pies is totally acceptable.)

Here are some suggested activities with blended families that don't require money or electricity: read books, start to write a book together, play musical instruments, plan a week's worth of healthy menus, go for a long walk, write letters (not emails) to friends, arrange photographs, organize unneeded clothes and household items into donation boxes for local charities, write in journals, visit neighbors, chart family trees (include pruned branches, if necessary), light candles, groom pets, and sit outside and appreciate nature. Be amazed at the positive energy that everyone feels after a fun family project.

During a recent snow storm, the schools were closed so I drove to stay with a few of my grandchildren while their parents were at work. A news report came on the radio seriously advising families about what to do with their children during the snow day. One particularly astute recommendation was: go play in the snow. Really? Does that come with instructions? Can it be done without a cell phone? Do the gloves need to match the hat? Somehow, we survived just fine.

~

Traveling Beyond the Farm

My love for travel came at an early age when the journey from our isolated farmhouse into town became a grand adventure. Town was only two miles away and had a population of only 1,000. But to me, the experience promised adventures and action. Everyone had to be clean and dressed in town clothes which meant no overalls, no barn boots, and no bare chests. To this day, I honor those rules every time I travel.

One summer day we piled into the station wagon and drove past the rolling fields to Wendell. Mom left us at the Tastee Freeze while she ran errands. I ordered a chocolate-dipped vanilla ice cream cone and sat outside on top of a picnic table. Other kids rode past on their bicycles and I nodded confidently as the Table Top Rebel of Gooding County. Within an hour, my brothers were wrestling in the dirt with rowdy playmates while I formed a club with some goofy girls who wandered by and wanted something to do. Our mission was to create and act in a spectacular play that would bring culture and refinement to Wendell. That was no small task.

We assigned parts and plotted the drama while determining that each one would rotate having the lead part. Then we invited the dirty boys over to watch our production. Just about the time I was presenting my great and glorious soliloquy, my mother drove up and hollered for us to get in the car. I accepted the interruption only because the next stop was the library. I waved farewell to the acting troupe while my mother muttered and brushed dirt off the boys. Then we went to the library and were allowed ten minutes to pick out five books while my mother returned the ones we had read. The pressure was intense. I ran to my favorite sections and selected some Nancy Drew mysteries, anything by Mark Twain, and a travel book. My brothers chose books about war and farm equipment. I already had read a chapter by the time we arrived home.

I loved travel books because I wanted to learn about places I could only imagine. That night at dinner I announced that someday I would travel the world. My father looked up and said that was nice but in the morning I needed to travel to the south forty acres and hoe some potatoes.

My first grand travel adventure profoundly impacted my life. As a 19-year-old college student, I sang soprano in the Vandaleer Concert Choir at the University of Idaho. We were invited to tour five countries in Europe to sing in elaborate cathedrals and in quaint village churches. Our repertoire included classics from J.S. Bach, Franz Schubert, Samuel Barber, and Stephen Foster. Final planning for the trip made me so nervous that I developed a serious case of shingles. I arrived late to the bus, smothered in gooey cream and itching like crazy.

"Can you make this trip?" asked Mr. Lockery, the serious, fatherly choir director.

"Yes, I can!" I said through clenched teeth.

There were 58 participants on the trip, 42 singers, 10 musicians, and six staff personnel. Most of the students had never been outside of Idaho. We landed at Heathrow International Airport in London and stepped into our own storybook. At the first rehearsal, my shingles disappeared as we sang "There is a Balm in Gilead" and the words and the music soothed the pain. I still love that song, and even though now I sing like an old toad I can hum the melody.

Our group was divided into two busses for the month-long tour. One bus carried the serious musicians and more sophisticated musical artists. I was not on that bus. I joined the freaks on the scalawag wagon and we laughed and hooted our way throughout Europe, ever mindful that once we stepped out of the bus we were official "ambassadors of good will abroad" and we had the embossed declaration by Governor Cecil Andrus to prove it.

The proclamation stated that we were to represent Idaho, and through the universal language of music we would improve human understanding and contribute to the making of a better world. I don't know if we improved anything, but we had damn good time. A few of the singers over-achieved in creating harmony and several babies were born nine months later. I chose not to go that route but focused on making merry in other ways at every opportunity.

In Darmstadt, Germany I stayed with a host family that didn't speak English and I didn't speak German. We choreographed an elaborate method of communication by using hand gestures, photographs, and translation books.

Mostly, we ate and drank. They offered beer with dinner so like any good guest I agreed to imbibe and did my part to foster good will between nations.

One afternoon they took me on an excursion into the mountains. Six of us crammed into an automobile the size of a clown car and we took off speeding down the autobahn. I almost lost my steamed dumplings when I noticed the speedometer indicated 150. Still astute enough to calculate meters, I realized that was only 93 miles an hour. I often drove that fast on the open freeways back home, but not in a crowded car careening around curves and between bulky trucks. They noticed my white knuckles and laughed hearty and loud. Silly Germans.

We survived the excursion and I still have the photograph of us standing on a bridge: Papa in a top coat and beret, Mama wearing a wool knit suit and feathered fedora, the quiet teenage son hiding behind his long hair, the solemn neighbor who acted as a poor translator, and the young daughter who asked if she could come back to America with me. For one afternoon in the village of Rüdesheim we were a good family that couldn't communicate. I felt right at home.

The Vandaleers toured five countries and presented 11 concerts. In Luxembourg we were invited to perform for the ambassador at the US Embassy. When we arrived at the embassy, Mr. Lockery came to each bus to deliver a stern admonishment: behave, sing well, or be on the next airplane home. He spent a long time at our bus, giving each one a stare that combined conviction and pure terror. We marched into the embassy, straightened our backs, opened our mouths, and sounded like a professional chorale of master musicians.

After the performance, the director fought back tears. And we did, too.

For our final concert, we sang in the American Cathedral in Paris, France. To this day I get emotional when I remember the magnificent sound in the ornate church. The acoustics were so profound that a sneeze was pure melody. When we finished the last strains of Bach's *Cantata No. 4,* there wasn't a dry eye in the entire choir. Even the freaks on the scalawag wagon were momentarily humbled. I had been working in my father's potato fields the summer before college and there I was, singing in a cathedral in Paris. The City of Light was light years away from the simple, sun-kissed pastures of home.

The next day we flew back to Idaho and tried to assimilate with those who hadn't sung in Coventry Cathedral in London, climbed to the second floor of the Eiffel Tower in Paris, stared at naked ladies in windows in Amsterdam, or trembled in fear as snarling armed guards entered our bus in East Berlin. The trip changed my life, and I vowed that I wouldn't remain down on the farm. Not when I could see and experience the world.

Since then, I've traveled to 32 countries. In the early days of not having enough money to buy gas to drive downtown, I discovered ways to get cheap trips or to go free as a chaperone or volunteer guide. I was elected to the board of the University of Idaho alumni association, and later became the board's president. That position allowed me to act as a paid host on alumni trips. I went to Ireland and Spain and all I had to do was be cheerful and helpful. A trained seal would do that for a free vacation.

I included my college-age daughter on the trip to

Spain. On a free day, we rented a car and drove to the Mediterranean Coast. We had a delightful time, especially because she was fluent in Spanish. Sometimes she would tell a joke in Spanish to the waiter and he would look at me and laugh hysterically. But, it was just her way of getting back at me for chaperoning her high school trip to Europe years earlier. She was mortified that I tagged along, but they needed another adult to go. How could I refuse?

I've taken trips alone, or as part of a couple, and/or with the family. Each option has benefits and challenges. A few years ago, I decided to plan a trip for my grown children, their spouses, their five children, Studley, and me. With such a large entourage, I decided to obtain assistance from a travel agency. I found a shop in the mall and wasted time looking through the advertisements that featured glossy photos of deliriously happy families laughing together on vacation. I remembered that these people were paid strangers and would never see each other again let alone share a suitcase and a missed flight connection. Families who travel together and come back with all the kids and are still speaking to each other are a rare and precious breed.

I finally arranged the details online and managed to coordinate the vacation for eleven family members. We were like a football team but without the private jet. Our mission was to leave the country, have a splendid time, and return alive. Touchdown and score!

Here are some key points I considered when attempting a family vacation:

- **Plan ahead.** We made reservations for hotel and airline tickets seven months in advance. Even with advance planning, we were all scrambling to get packed a few hours before departure. We don't worry about boarding animals because we only have Koi fish, and they hibernate through the winter. They're the perfect pets, and they'll never stain the carpet.

- **Get or update passports if leaving the country.** One dilemma: My son and his wife had a new baby, but she still needed a passport. The rules state that no one else can be in the passport photo, so he had to hold up her tiny body with one hand. She looks like a puppet on a stick, and that passport is good for five years.

- **Pack lightly.** Studley and I just roll up hand-washable clothes and travel with carryon bags only. Of course, parents with kids need twenty extra pieces of luggage just for diapers and electronic gear. Traveling light is just another advantage of being older, and we won't need diapers or sippy cups for a few more years.

- **Include workout shoes and clothes.** Most hotels have gyms so we could exercise before and after enjoying insane quantities of piña coladas and nachos. And walking in the sand along the beach really tones the legs as we ambled into town for some coconut gelato.

- **Plan separate activities.** Studley and I left to golf one day, and we rode horses on the beach another day. The other adults shared babysitting duties so each couple could relax without bringing a pacifier or an animated puppet show. Then we all got together for meals and playing on the beach. Don't spend too much money on expensive excursions and organized children's activities, because the kids will get the most delight out of watching the tide fill in their footprints in the sand.

- **Get professional photographs.** It sounds cheesy, but the resorts do a good job of organizing family photographs. We're pleased with the results because our phones just don't take quality photos. We also want documented proof that everyone was having fun. Or else!

- **There will be some drama.** At any given time, at least one of the five children was crying, pouting, or attempting to run away. But after a few margaritas, the adults didn't care.

- **One important rule of life: enjoy the beauty of the moment.** We stayed at a lovely resort on the beach in Los Cabos, Mexico. A week later, I could still hear the laughter of my granddaughters playing in the waves, feel the motion of the ocean, taste the delicious fresh sea bass dinner, and visualize the full moon reflecting over the water. We'll savor those memories and use them as a catalyst for planning the next trip. But first we need to work off the extra ten pounds so we can party again.

I often think about the Wendell Library and the travel books that sparked my youthful imagination and wanderlust. If my father were still alive, I would run and tell him that I've been to Paris twice. He'd probably look up and calmly say that was nice, and now go to work. Or, maybe he would put down his newspaper, pull up a chair, and say, "Tell me about it!" That by itself would be a unique, uncharted experience and one worth exploring.

~

The Proper Care and Coddling
of Curmudgeons

I see old people. They're everywhere. And there's one looking back at me in the mirror. Just yesterday, I was cruising down the road in my 1972 Firebird swaying to some saucy songs from Carole King's *Tapestry* album blaring on my 8-track stereo, and now I'm driving a sturdy SUV to the drugstore to buy Geritol and Metamucil.

Somehow the world did a fast-forward through several decades, and I'm trying to remember where I put my bearings. I vaguely remember tucking my sweet babies into bed, and suddenly they appeared at my door with my grandkids. I don't recognize the old woman in my mirror.

According to the Census Bureau, 21 percent of Americans will be at least sixty-five years old by 2050. And the younger generation is having fewer children, so there won't be workers (or jobs) to fund programs to take care of old people. But by then I'll be ninety-nine years old and won't care. Just prop me in the sunshine, put a straw in a jug of wine, leave a plate of soft cheese and bread, and play some jazz. If I get cranky, just kiss my aging attitude and leave me alone.

Business analysts predict that all of us old folks will generate profitable new markets for products and supplies. Investors are eager to find opportunities connected to strategic demographic trends, and entrepreneurs are focusing on how to capitalize on the needs and demands of the older generation.

I can save them a lot of complicated scheming and precious time by offering some good old common sense. And it's free. Here are the top investment strategies from my organization called OFF—Old Fart's Foundation:

- **Buy stock in drugstores.** There's always a line at the prescription counter at Walgreens, and the kindly pharmacists usually explain the drugs. "Yes, ma'am, this could make you poop in your pants, but your other ailments will disappear."

- **Invest in makers of medical devices.** We could have a one-stop boutique where we have our hair and nails done and go home with a new hip and pacemaker. Ideally, these devices would be installed in the proper locations on our bodies. And, like any good nail and hair salon, the humorous staff would ply the clientele with complimentary wine.

- **Honor the blue chip companies of your long-ago youth.** Johnson & Johnson still makes Band-Aids, creams, and potions, and for now the world headquarters remain in New Jersey. Buy soon before some foreign conglomerate takes over and then you'll need a translator to read the directions for applying a Band-Aid. And don't trust any novice interpreter when deciphering the difference between face lotion and hemorrhoid creams or you could tighten more than you need.

- **Invest in a single-story home** and stay there as long as you can still organize happy hour and find the bathroom.

Our generation is full of dreamers, travelers, poets, and activists. We charted new paths and have the scars from battles won and lost. Now it's our time to relax and enjoy the last third of life with quiet satisfaction. Unless, of course, there's a party with a live band. Then we'll get fancy and go dancing.

Even with dance parties and cocktails, we still get stressed and overtired. When that happens, it's perfectly acceptable to escape. When life gets too heavy to handle, there is only one solution to end this misery. Run away. You can plan your escape on a whim or take several months to organize the scheme. These are a few of my favorites, and the first requirement is that you turn off your cell phone. Yes, you must.

- **The Spontaneous, Easy, and Cheap Fling.** This option brings new meaning to the term "nooner." If you only have an hour, bring your lunch to work and leave at noon. If you have a car, play some rhythm and blues and drive to a park. If you don't have transportation, listen to music on your iPod and walk slowly to the nearest quiet space. Just sit there, munch on your food (include at least one cookie), and then close your eyes. Do nothing but meditate as you listen to the music. I suggest some jazz or songs from Broadway musicals. Then return to work refreshed and rejuvenated without feeling the urge to send a snarky email or trash your cubicle.

- **The Delightful Day Break.** Take a vacation day just for yourself and mark it on the calendar a month in advance. Hike in the hills, read a book, write a short story, plant some flowers, or if your budget allows, spend a few hours at the local spa. By the end of the blissful day, expect some immediate crisis involving at least one of your children, your elderly parent, or your plumbing. But you'll be pleasant, positive, and ready for any emergency. No sedatives required.

- **The Total Indulgent Escape.** Recently, I ran away to New York City. I'm a volunteer member of a board that was meeting, but I wasn't planning to attend. There had been a death in the family, I moved my invalid mother to a different assisted living facility, a relative called and yelled at me, I got the Head Cold from Hell, there were problems with a book I was publishing, and I gained five pounds. So I did the only thing that made sense: I bought a discounted flight and left for the city.

A farmer's daughter from Idaho going to New York City is similar to Dorothy seeing the Emerald City in *The Wizard of Oz.* Humming "Somewhere Over the Rainbow," I hit the Big Apple running as if being chased by flying monkeys. In three days, I attended the meeting, laughed until I snorted at the hilarious Broadway musical *The Book of Mormon,* toured the Steinway piano factory, meandered through the Metropolitan Museum of Art, took a solemn trip to Ground Zero, watched a performance at Lincoln Center, and ate and drank fabulous food and wine.

On the last evening, two friends and I found Nizza Bar a Vin Italienne, a delightful Italian wine bar, and sat outside consuming fresh gnocchi, shrimp salad, and crusty bread. Of course, we consumed a bottle of Barbera wine presented by a perky waitress who was determined to become a Broadway star. We watched as police closed the street and a crew prepared a movie scene for Liam Neeson. My runaway excursion was the perfect remedy.

Studley, my heroic and understanding husband, was waiting at the airport, and we hugged and kissed like long-lost lovers. Then he asked if I wanted to go find a place for dinner. I shook my head and said, "There's no place like home."

After returning home from a trip, I believe that the best way to start a new day, after some festive canoodling, is to make coffee, grab the newspaper, and read the obituaries.

Reading about dead people causes me to contemplate the summary of my life. Most of us are somewhere between "convicted felon" and "millionaire philanthropist." For an interesting assignment, I find some random obituaries and read about what happened to people between birth and death. Sometimes I write my own. Whatever the story will be, I want to make it sassy enough so others will say, "What a grand life she had!"

Many, many years ago, to earn my degree in journalism from the University of Idaho, my last requirement was to complete an internship at the *Lewiston Tribune*. I eagerly anticipated that I would write compelling, award-winning feature stories to be published on the front page under my huge byline. Instead, I was assigned to write obituaries.

The job did not require talent in creative writing, investigative journalism, or serious analysis. My task was to condense a person's life to a few paragraphs, spell the name correctly, and include funeral details. Initially, I resented the assignment, but I soon grew to appreciate the information and anecdotes about the dearly departed. I often imagined extra details about who they were and what they did. A few times I fabricated interesting facts for the published obituary. The families never complained.

Now when I begin each morning with coffee and the newspaper, I read the front page, swear about politics, and then turn to the obituaries. I study the smiling faces of strangers, and I calculate how many were younger than I am. Then I read their stories. The older people have the best obituaries because they often include fascinating facts about being rugged pioneers, former ballerinas, independent cowboys, brave soldiers, happy homemakers, or those who fought courageous battles with cancer and now sing with the angels.

The short obituaries cause me to wonder why the person had only one paragraph of life worth mentioning. Maybe no one knew the hobbies, adventures, and family that might have been. Maybe the survivors didn't want to pay for a longer article. Or maybe that's what the person wanted, and who am I to question why there were no funeral services?

When I conduct writing workshops for teenagers, I often advise them to write their own obituaries. After an initial hesitation, they get to work and usually produce confident predictions of being the future president, inventor, movie star, or football hero. Their long and happy lives will be full of grand adventures, and then a park or building will be named after them in honor of their contributions to society. Their cockiness is contagious.

When I do the same assignment with middle-aged women, the results are different. Their imagined obituaries focus on family, travels with their spouse, and jobs, in order. By midlife, the youthful desire to save the planet evolves into the more attainable goal to be the best volunteer at a local charity, to retire from a productive career, or to be celebrated as an unforgettable, lovable grandmother.

Occasionally we'll read an obituary about people we knew and loved. The best way to honor their memory is to get busy living the extra days we've been given that they didn't have. Carpe diem.

Another good personal goal is to avoid death by hyperbole. Middle-aged women are entitled to an occasional Snark Attack so they can stomp on civility and ridicule annoying behavior. This happened recently as I was reading messages on Facebook and then indignantly scoffed at some of the dramatic and ridiculous hyperbole. Because I live to serve, here is some wise advice for dealing with the top ten examples of egregious exaggerations.

- **To die for!** Someone wrote that she saw some shoes to die for. Even a minimal amount of astute observation would conclude that if the person really died, then she couldn't wear the shoes. Plus, the sentence ended in a preposition, which is the absolute worst grammatical error in the entire world! Don't have friends who offer to die for shoes or dessert.

- **I'm starving!** Usually untrue. Some who make that comment could live for weeks on the leftover junk food stashed in their cars.

- **Share this message or burn in hell!** Never send or forward these threats. When it's time for my Final Judgment Day, there is an enormous list of transgressions and trespasses for which I need atonement. Those times I didn't share a Facebook message won't even make the top one hundred.

- **She lost a ton of weight!** No she didn't, unless she weighed over 2,000 pounds. If she really did, then by all means celebrate with her.

- **This is the worst day ever!** Au contraire, sweet cheeks. There will be days that are horrific in comparison to today, just as there will be glorious days in the future. That's life.

- **Men suck!** Well, sometimes they do. And sometimes women do, too.

- **Mondays suck!** Hey, you're employed, and there are many people who would take your job in a heartbeat. Stop whining and get to work.

- **If this won't make you cry, you don't have a heart.** Wrong. I have a heart because I'm alive to read this and it didn't make me cry. I don't want to feel heartless, so I won't read such items anymore.

- **OMG!** This abbreviation for "Oh, my God!" should be used only for events of biblical magnitude. Watching a vampire movie doesn't qualify.

- **Cutest Puppy (Kitten, Grandchild, Prom Dress, Gall Bladder) Ever!** No, not really. But I'll smile at all your family photos and then post some of my own just to prove how cute some grandkids can be.

After pontificating about exaggerated expressions, my Snark Attack disappeared for a week or so. I returned to reading the many messages and posts from friends and associates, secure in the knowledge that we would never criticize or mock each other's messages. Except for the note from a dieting friend who said she was hungry enough to eat a horse. I almost died laughing over that one.

And as long as we're discussing pet peeves, why not talk about breastfeeding? I think it's fine, as long as it's expressed in good taste. (Rim shot.)

I recently attended an elegant wedding at a seaside resort where the gift table and the guests were well-endowed. However, there was some engorged indignation at the reception as two perky women nursed their babies without discreetly covering the bobbing heads of the darling sucklings. One of the bridesmaids conveniently wore a strapless gown to easier facilitate the moveable feast.

Reaction to the public display of liberal lactation ranged from frothed and pumped-up annoyance to flowing praise for the natural and healthy nourishment between the mother and child reunion. It sucks to be criticized for using a supply-on-demand device for its original purpose.

"Oh, my, I must warn Harold not to go over there," a woman muttered to a group of older guests with permed hair, lace hankies, and sensible shoes. "I haven't seen this many bare breasts since I watched a National Geographic documentary about African tribes."

"In my day, we discreetly fed our babies under a blanket, and my mother hired a nurse maid for her children," snorted another lady. "Things were more civilized back then when we could ship off the kids to boarding schools."

They murmured, nodded their heads, and clucked their tongues. Meanwhile, Harold and his buddies were sneaking peeks around the corner and clutching their sunken chests as faint mammary memories dribbled into their thoughts.

The younger crowd seemed nonchalant and didn't latch onto the uncomfortable tension that leaked into the room. They laughed the night away, draining jugs of wine until they acted like boobs. To insure that the event wasn't a total bust, they danced through the spot so the hooters could hoot, the knockers could knock, and the stranded friends could wean themselves away from the dried-up and sagging patrons. In a final tit-for-tat, the young adults pulled the older folks out of their bondage and onto the dance floor to lift and separate their drooping spirits.

By then, the contented babies were asleep and the milked mothers had a few hours to pad themselves and dance the Fandango until the cows came home. That way, they could have their wedding cake and eat it, too.

The best formula for enjoying a special occasion that involves young couples is to anticipate the appearance of at least one nursing mother. Offended people can choose to avert their attention to the drunken uncle who always crashes the party. No one demands that he should hide in the bathroom but he's far more offensive than boobs. The public nursing only lasts a few minutes, and the alternative is to hear a screaming baby and witness a swollen mother in pain.

I nursed my two babies each for a year, and it was a rewarding experience. I never walked around in public hooked up to the little buggers, but I don't disapprove of those who do. There are far too many neglected babies who hunger for the affection and attachment of loving mothers.

And speaking of mothers, mine came from a generation overly consumed with underwear and accidents. When our mothers admonished us to wear clean underwear just in case we were in an accident, we dutifully obeyed for fear that during an emergency the medical personnel would rush to our rescue but suddenly stop tending to our injuries. "Look, Bob, this one isn't wearing clean underwear," we imagined the EMT muttering in disgust. "Let 'er bleed out."

A recent experience caused me to reevaluate my lackadaisical commitment to the strict rules of wearing underwear. The event that must never be mentioned again happened in front of a posh day spa. I was in an accident—but the underwear wasn't an issue because I wasn't wearing any.

A few special times each year, I treat myself to a hot stone massage at a spa just ten minutes from my house. To avoid unnecessary dressing and undressing, I slip on baggy sweatpants, an oversized sweater, flip-flops, and a hat and drive to the spa. Easy in, easy out.

After a wonderful ninety-minute session, complete with lavender-infused oils, eucalyptus aromatherapy, and a brain-numbing scalp massage, I donned my innocuous outfit and sauntered to my car. Still relaxed, I put the car in reverse and promptly bumped into the UPS van parked behind me. Talk about a rude awakening! My dreamlike aura shattered into an ugly nightmare.

I jumped out of the car, clutching oily arms across my unsecured chest, and rushed back to the van. The driver, of course, was a handsome young stud juggling boxes of potions and lotions for the beautiful people who pranced in and out of the spa. My greasy hair resembled the matted hide of a swamp rat, my frumpy sweatpants clung to my freshly oiled skin, and I suddenly became acutely aware that I could double as an itinerant bag lady.

"I'm sorry, ma'am," he said. "I shouldn't have parked behind you."

I resisted the urge to call him "boy" and swallowed my pride about being called "ma'am." My pride tasted strangely like lavender.

We surveyed the scene and couldn't see any damage to either vehicle. The only injury was to my self-confidence. He smiled, took one last confused look at me, and then moved his van. By now a group of interested beautiful people watched from inside the spa. I lowered my head, shuffled to the car, looked both ways, and then drove away. I won't return for several years.

I'm becoming concerned that my mirror doesn't work. When my eyesight weakened, I purchased a new lighted mirror with a 10X magnification so I could apply mascara without guessing the actual location of my eyelashes. The first time I looked into the mirror, I screamed and jumped back in horror because there was a ghastly old woman staring back at me! I want my money—and my face—returned!

The illuminated, colossal reflection exaggerated the erratic road map of lines, wrinkles, and crevices that sprouted around my eyes like jagged lightning bolts surrounding deep, bloodshot sinkholes. Why didn't someone tell me my face resembled a damp shirt that had been forgotten in the dryer? At least my friends also have failing eyesight, so they may not even notice.

I flipped the mirror over to the normal view and was relieved because my poor vision couldn't detect any flaws. I prefer that side now. For security and insecurity purposes, I have taped a warning label to the magnified side of the mirror.

It's called a vanity mirror for a reason, but I refuse to channel my inner queen of the *Snow White* movie and ask the mirror on the wall who is the fairest one of all. I know the answer, and not even a flamboyant skit by the jolly seven dwarfs could make me laugh now because that would just add more unwanted lines.

After surviving the shock of magnified reality, I looked again at my eyes. These green orbs have been dilated, examined, and corrected since I was ten years old. They have peered from dozens of ugly frames that included cat-eyes with rhinestones, black square nerd glasses, and delicate rimless beauties that cost a month's mortgage and broke every time I sneezed. My eyes survived surgery for holes in both retinas and continued to work after a failed attempt at laser treatment. Best of all, these irreplaceable body parts have allowed me to write and read books and to see the wonders of the world.

These eyes cried with joy when I held my precious babies, widened with amazement when I visited 32 countries around the world, leaked buckets over physical and mental pain, and focused with passion as I stared into my husband's loving eyes. Six decades of visions are stored within my memories as on-demand movies after a life full of adventure, tears, and laughter that I have been privileged to see and experience. I have earned each and every line around these well-worn eyes, and I intend to earn many more.

At the next family dinner, I'll don my newest pair of spectacles and prepare the list and check favorite recipes. I'll imagine the cacophony coming from the children's table as I witness the generations gathered around the tables squabbling over the last piece of pie. With the blessed ability to see, I'll give thanks for the abundant vision before me. And then I'll grab the pie.

Another reason never to use a magnified mirror is that your chin hairs will resemble a Chia pet. The world is under assault from wars and rumors of wars, illness, crime, weather calamities, and Internet photos of Walmart shoppers. But what really causes anguish to most middle-aged women is to discover coarse, industrial-strength hairs on their chins.

These unwanted and unsightly growths often are strong enough to be woven into nets to transport military tanks. And they usually erupt in two seconds and protrude six inches before we're even aware they're fouling our faces. That's why we always carry lighted mirrors and pliers in our purse, right next to the flask.

In my book *Menopause Sucks* (gratuitous plug), I wrote that untended black hairs on your chin will make you resemble a Brillo pad, and you'll need to bribe your grandkids for a hug. Blame the problem on hormones and genetics. These two culprits—along with politicians and bad lighting—usually are responsible for most of your problems.

You can't do a darned thing about heredity. If your ancestors came from the Scandinavian countries, you may never need to shave your legs, and you could have a full beard of fine fuzz and no one would notice. However, if your people came from southern Europe, you've been shaving since you were ten years old and have a five o'clock shadow by lunchtime. You like to eat meat, and sometimes you cook it first.

As for the hormone issues, you can control them with proper medication, meditation, and massive amounts of merlot. Hair follicles are extremely sensitive to imbalances of hormones, and your internal estrogen and progesterone factories are rioting and sending baffling signals to the hair-growth office in your brain. Then the hair on your head begins to fall out until your once-thick pelt resembles a dog with mange. Don't worry; the hair will reappear on your chin and toes. This causes stress, and stress exacerbates hair loss. At this stage, the quality of life depends upon your sense of humor and your motivation to get out of bed.

During menopause, you may notice other changes to your hair. My hair was wavy, so to get the popular straight styles, I would curl my hair around used orange juice cans, which made for a troublesome night's sleep and a sticky buildup on my Herman's Hermits pillowcases. After I entered menopause, I started growing someone else's hair. It's dry and thick in the back and so thin on top that my head often shines like the Chrysler Building. I'm giddy to wake up every morning and still have hair to comb. My doctor said it was thyroid issues, but in my age-induced confusion, I thought she said hemorrhoid problems. That cream didn't help my hair at all.

To fight hair loss, you can try several products that are available without prescription. These topical ointments take at least six months to activate, so you have time to enjoy other symptoms of age that include hot flashes, mood swings, incontinence, memory lapses, weight gain, sleep problems, and adult acne. The fact that we survive at all is a true testament to our strength, resolve, and refusal to quietly go away.

For middle-aged women, every day brings new opportunities for humiliation, the kind that comes when you laugh and wet your pants at the same time, usually in a business meeting. Recently, I was preparing for minor dental surgery when I noticed a mini-redwood growing from my chin that had the dangerous potential to distract the dentist as he was using sharp tools in my mouth. The stubborn hair was rooted in my ribcage, so I attacked it with tweezers until there was a huge, bloody hole in my chin. It was winter so I couldn't blame the wound on a mosquito bite. I slathered on some Bag Balm to stop the bleeding and then applied perfume to hide the ointment's pungent smell. I hurried into the office and plopped down on the dental recliner. That's when I noticed my black boots didn't match. I heard the dental assistants snickering behind their protective masks. Then the doctor appeared with a twenty-foot needle.

"I'll be in a lot of pain," I moaned. "Do you have anything to help me?"

I vaguely remember being drenched in numbness. I didn't know if it came from a painkiller shot or from laughing gas. I really didn't care.

~

A Time to Laugh,
a Time to Get a Weapon

The Book of Ecclesiastes in the Holy Bible was written more than two thousand years ago, just before I was born. Chapter III contains the famous verses about there being a time, a season, and a purpose for everything. Who needs modern self-help books and expensive therapy when this astute advice explains it all?

In the late 1950s, Pete Seeger adapted the words from Ecclesiastes to write the song "Turn! Turn! Turn!" The most popular rendition was performed by The Byrds in 1965, and I fondly remember singing the tune as I rode my horse in the country. The song included the words from the Bible verses, ending with "A time for peace." Seeger added six words: "I swear it's not too late." After the worldwide popularity of the song, he later remarked that he received too much credit for only writing six words.

Over the years, I've read various books and watched videos that promise to provide all the answers. Just put it out there! Expect and visualize greatness! Here is the secret! All this advice is encouraging and motivational until you lose your job to the company trollop. Then all the good vibrations, humming, and drumming won't stop your sorrow. That's when a good cry is not only tolerated but expected.

A few times, I've gone beyond the weeping stage and visualized smashing something and/or someone with a hammer. The most recent example of imaginary vindication relates to the embarrassing fact that I was swindled by a local businessman whom I thought was a friend. I resent the loss of tens of thousands of dollars, but mostly I'm chagrined at the reality that I'm not as smart as I thought. The retaliatory hammer swings both ways.

To compound the humiliation, this isn't the first time I've lost money to con artists. Maybe it will get easier after the funds are all gone. I'll write the last check to that nice man from Nigeria because he promised a 200 percent return on investment.

After being swindled, it was easy to get bitter and distrustful. But that's no fun. As many advice gurus accurately note, being angry at someone only allows the jerk to live rent-free in my head. There are abundant memories and triumphant visions that fit much better into my mind, and they don't leave a scowl on my face or lead to prison.

Call it a case of sour grapes. More like forty-five cases. I was bamboozled for booze by a former friend who solicited money for an exclusive wine club. Red flags were slapping me in the face, but I couldn't see beyond my rosé-colored glasses.

I don't enjoy broadcasting my stupidity, but I hope my mistake can prevent other women from being swindled by shady shysters. The guy sold a snake oil deal disguised in a wine bottle, so of course I willingly imbibed in his exciting new venture known as Vinemakers LLC. (Note: in this ca. Limited Liability means the managing partner didn't need to honor the contract. This is why sometimes we need and should use lawyers to save us from ourselves.)

The result of being a sucker: I lost more than $30,000 and now have 540 bottles of unlabeled wine without foil over the corks. My house resembles a moonshine shack.

The wine is good—it received a 90-point rating from *Wine Spectator*—but not worth $56 a bottle. I can't sell the wine because I'm not a distributor and it's not labeled. My only options are to give it away at charity functions and to throw raucous parties. So come on over and step through the boxes and bottles. I'll be in the corner wearing a dunce hat. But, at least I'll have a nice buzz to go with it.

As a sobering public service, I now am qualified to offer the top five ways I will use from now on to avoid bad investments:

- **Be skeptical.** Most middle-aged women have a tendency to believe and trust a friend whose LinkedIn profile virtually claims he's the smartest man in the entire business world. Big mistake. I was duped, and there's nothing I can do about it, except create a Certificate of Higher Learning from Mistakes and hang it on my wall.

- **Ask to see financial statements and details about other investors.** I learned too late that I invested three times more money than the others. Most of the victims were women, but there was one man who doesn't want to be identified because he's a local financial advisor. Every investor lost at least $10,000, and the winemaker eventually lost her house. Sometimes it's difficult to believe that crooks could take advantage of fun-loving, educated women, but we're an easy target. We were raised to be pleasers. I'm over that now.

- **Have a non-related lawyer review any contract.** For my $30,000 investment, I was given a document that "guaranteed" a return of capital participation, an additional 15 percent profit sharing on all the wine sold, and six cases of wine annually. The club went out of business, and there was no legal recourse to enforce the bogus claims. We were offered cases of wine, and that's all. My forty-five cases were delivered from the back of a pickup truck on a 100-degree day, and the "Seasoned Senior Executive with Global Marketing Experience" was nowhere in sight to help unload. His subsequent emails promising to "make all of you whole" only succeeded in making all of us a whole lot angrier.

- **Know the legal options.** I couldn't squeeze dollars from a barrel of fermented grapes, so I didn't try to sue. The winery doesn't have the money to pay the debts, so all I would get would be legal bills that could lead me to drink. More. It's also illegal to physically harm the guy who cheated me. I already researched that option, and I don't have any time to go to jail.

- **Appreciate my own values.** If I asked my friends, associates, and their parents for investment money, and then the project failed, I would work multiple jobs to pay back the investors. But slimy skunks don't agree with that philosophy. They could, however, be ridiculed someday in a book. I'll be sure to send him a copy.

My final words of advice: Don't avoid future risks, but research any financial venture and know that if it's too good to be true, it's a lie. Finally, keep a sense of humor when faced with negative situations. For my pending party, I will have an altered game of Pin the Tail on the Donkey. Guess whose photograph is strategically placed?

I don't remember classes in school that taught us how to avoid crooks. I do remember that most of my teachers wanted to retire after I was in their class. A few were moved to a pleasant rest home in the country.

I'd like to offer a thanks and an apology to my former teachers and to remind other teachers that their labors are not in vain. Someday, maybe forty years from now, they will receive a thank you and/or apology from former students who have succeeded in life without serving time in jail or randomly texting photos of their genitalia.

I attended twelve years of public school in the village of Wendell, Idaho, and some of my teachers also instructed my parents at the same school a generation earlier. My teachers taught me the proper use of "your" and "you're," how to find the seven continents on a map, and what practical skills I needed to get good jobs. It was common-sense education without a "Caught You Being Good" award, and I'd like to thank them for their guidance and apologize for being so obnoxious.

I was *that* kid. The incorrigible class clown, the goofy girl making the most noise, and the jolly jester singing during exams. Instead of numbing me with medication (thank you!), the teachers, including a frustrated Mrs. Petersen, regularly sent me to the principal's office where I told jokes until they begged me to return to class. We were graded on "deportment," and a bad mark would keep a good student off of the published Honor Roll. I always earned honor grades but usually received an F in behavior. But I was the school newsletter editor, so I just returned my name to the list.

In fifth grade, Mrs. Gates daily rapped on my desk because I was staring out of the window. I explained to her that I was daydreaming about imaginary adventures, so she told me to write short stories. As a published author, I'm grateful for that assignment. In sixth grade, Mrs. Dennis would shake her head at my antics before she sent me to her husband, the principal. Mr. Webster, my junior high band teacher, once shouted at me that I wasn't funny. I retorted that really, I was! All the students laughed, just to prove me right.

My true heroes were my English teachers. In junior high, Mrs. Coffman drilled me about how to conjugate a verb, spell correctly, and diagram a sentence. In high school, Miss Luke told me I was a good writer, and she explained poetry in terms of meter, rhythm, and iambic tetrameter. She advised me to read works by great storytellers including Mark Twain, Louisa May Alcott, and Agatha Christie. I adored Miss Luke but lost contact with her after I left high school. I've always wondered where she lived after Wendell because I want to send her a poem written in perfect iambic pentameter.

To these and other memorable teachers, I say a hearty thank you for all that I learned from their instructions, advice, and example. And to all of those I irritated, I humbly apologize. Finally, to Mr. Webster wherever you are: I'm still funny!

The school of hard knocks is never fun, but it usually adds to our knowledge of the world, the good, the bad, and the potentially lethal. Some of you have been around the block enough times to know where to avoid the mud and dog poop or when to stop and smell the roses. Others, however, refuse to try a better path, so they continue to trip over the same obstacles. And, then there is THAT group—the ones who stand in the street waiting for a free ride and then can't understand why they get hit by a bus.

My spirited and splendid journey through life has taught me that the secrets to survival can be condensed to five easy paragraphs. It's short because so is life.

- **Use your common sense.** Spend less money than you make or you'll become a slave to debt, which leads to misery, failure, and regret. Don't go on a zip line through the jungle if you have a bladder problem because there aren't any restrooms on those wobbly platforms. If you regularly eat an entire pecan pie with ice cream, you won't look good naked. See how it works? Our brains have the remarkable ability to make good or bad decisions and choices. My mature brain tells me to manage money, avoid zip lines, and not go within ten miles of a dessert.

- **Focus on fitness.** Keep that pie image (and who wouldn't?) and acknowledge that input should balance output. If you consume more food than you need to survive, you should expend enough energy to burn off the unnecessary calories. Get and stay healthy because life has a way of instantly whisking you from the high school prom to your twenty-year reunion. And then it's just a few hours before you're sneaking into the store for reading glasses and incontinence supplies. Don't wait until you're older and lack the physical ability to skip with your grandchildren or chase your handsome hunk around the house, at different times of course.

- **Love to be in love.** As the years go by, there is a profound sweetness in waking up with someone who accepts your wrinkles, thinning hair, and sagging body parts and then says, "Good morning, gorgeous." Love your lover every day, from a passing wink to a sensual massage. A steady, exclusive relationship can turn a slow dance on the patio into a romantic encounter worthy of an evening in Paris. (Paris is always an adequate option.)

- **Bad things happen.** No one gets a free pass on calamity. During your life, you probably will experience flat tires, funerals, diarrhea, betrayal, lost love, fights with family, at least one broken bone, flatulence during a wedding, and the world's worst boss. So you get up again, adjust your armor, and holler that you're ready for the next challenge. Looking back at the assorted chaos in my life, I realize there were far more splendid times than bad. And the truly amazing adventures happened after I initially failed or took a risk.

- **Attitude is everything.** Positive, grateful people enjoy the best of life. By midlife, the laugh lines around their eyes reveal countless smiles through the miles, and their journey is one to emulate. Crabby, cynical worrywarts suck the energy from everyone they meet. Avoid them.

"Dear Abby" Pauline Phillips died at the age of ninety-four. For almost forty-six years, her advice columns appeared in 1,000 newspapers around the world. She wrote in her autobiography that her demanding job was not work because "It's only work if you'd rather be doing something else." I agree with her, and so my advice is to choose wisely, get healthy, love intensely, combat calamity, and be happy. I try to remember that life is short. So I'll make it sassy.

One of the best ways to learn about the world is to go beyond the travel books and take adventures on your own. There are many distinct ways to maneuver from here to there without appearing stupid. Confidence and brains win over high-heeled shoes and expensive luggage.

When I traveled solo on business trips more than thirty years ago, I experienced negative and skeptical reactions from hotel receptionists, waiters, and even other travelers. They assumed I was a loser who couldn't get a man to accompany me or a floozy looking for some action in the back of the lobby bar. I enjoyed proving them wrong.

Now women comprise more than 51 percent of people traveling for business and pleasure. Most of us have a routine when entering a hotel room. I have my room key ready so I don't need to fumble through my key-eating purse. I prop open the door with my suitcase and make low grumbling noises just in case someone is hiding in the bathroom. I check the closets and shower for bad guys, and have my hand in my pocket pretending I have a gun. Yes, I'm bad and no one should mess with me. I make mental notes if the bed looks clean, there is a coffee maker with coffee, and I can't detect the smell of cigarette smoke or animals. After approving the room, I close and lock the door. Wearing a holster and pistol is a good idea, but that usually is discouraged by law enforcement and doesn't look good with business suits.

While on a business trip, most women use their free time to (1) exercise in the hotel gym, (2) find the nearest wine bar, or (3) pretend they are comfortable browsing in Saks Fifth

Avenue. I usually combine all three by jogging past Saks into the nearest establishment that offers a dry cabernet.

On a recent visit to Phoenix, I stayed near an upscale mall, a place that according to the glossy brochure "pampers shoppers with a gardenlike ambiance." Eager to feel pampered, I scurried over after my business appointment. I felt perky and confident meandering into the mall and mingling with sophisticated women toting Coach and Louis Vuitton and wearing those fancy shoes with the red soles.

I muttered out loud when I spied a Ralph Lauren store. I'd give a month's salary to dress like the exquisite model in the RL ads, the tall, thin one with Rapunzel hair, boots to her thighs, and chiseled features, who lounges with a bevy of beautiful people in a pristine meadow beside magnificent horses. I sashayed into the store and was drawn to a lovely sweater that actually cost a month's salary. That wouldn't leave me any money for the jeans and boots, so I sauntered back out.

Next came Saks Fifth Avenue.

I grew up on a farm outside of Wendell, Idaho, population 1,000. The village had one general store called Simerly's with a slogan that said, "If we don't have it, you don't need it." Saks did not have this slogan on their ornate entrance. I went in anyway and immediately felt my confidence drain like air fizzling from a pricked balloon. My inner child begged to leave and find a store with more practical items such as a clown nose and a whoopee cushion.

I meandered about, trying to emulate the nonchalant attitude of the other shoppers, but those astute saleswomen could detect an imposter from a hundred yards. They were almost haughty in their demeanor, and I sensed that they were laughing at me. "Go back to the farm, sweetie. You don't belong here. And take last year's purse with you."

Most of us enjoy a little retail therapy, and we work so we have money to purchase items that we want and need. I believe in free enterprise and in the economic principles of supply and demand. Louis Vuitton wouldn't make $10,000 purses if they didn't have customers who could buy them. I also believe it's better to pay a down payment on a house instead of a purse, but that's just me.

In Saks, there was a special room just for Coach purses. They didn't have price tags, but you know when a bag is encased in a lighted and locked glass display box that it will cost more than your car. The elegant woman behind the counter smiled politely but didn't offer to show me anything. It was as if she suspected I still had manure on my shoes and my pickup truck was double-parked behind the feed store. Even with my lowly country girl intellect, I know it's dumb to spend thousands of dollars on a bag that's used to carry tampons, emergency candy, loose change, and outdated coupons.

I finally left without buying anything, mainly because I didn't want to spend the monthly mortgage on a pair of shoes that assumed only two inches of leather across the toes could support my ability to stand upright on four-inch heels. Next door I found a cute coffee shop that sold cupcakes with an amazing concept: they were split in the middle with a cream filling spread between the layers and not on the top. I sat outside and enjoyed my $20 latte and cupcake while I watched the people.

Every now and then, I spied a few kindred souls emerging sack-less from Saks. Without needing a mall directory, they would disappear into the shop and emerge with coffee and a sweet treat. Then they would find a bench and pretend to be pampered in the gardenlike ambiance. We all were poignant actors in our own morality play, trading Burberry for blueberry and Fendi for frosting. But we chose to savor the experience with every bite. We'll probably never live nor look like women who patronize the luxury stores, but we are best friends with the cupcake maker. She had it, and we needed it.

In the past, as a single female traveler, I was often seated in the back of the hotel restaurant as the pathetic loner and obvious loser. Waiters continually asked if I was waiting for someone, perhaps to offer hope to my solitude. Now I can confidently order a table for one and ask for the wine list, and no one calls the authorities to haul me away. My eighty-year-old widowed mother still refuses to go to a restaurant alone. My grown daughter entered a restaurant in Spain by herself and competently ordered in Spanish. Progress, indeed.

Here are some helpful tips for women who love to travel but choose to return alive.

- **Pack light and wear sensible shoes.** Be able to wrestle all your luggage by yourself and still run a city block, if necessary. Wear casual business attire and avoid stilettos unless you can use them as pointed weapons. Heels can be handy if you don't have a gun when first checking your room for bad guys.

- **Don't loop your purse over your head** because if some jerk wants to steal it, you'll be slammed to the ground in the process. Don't read maps or fiddle with your cell phone while standing alone because that makes you appear vulnerable. You need to look fierce enough to scare off any prospective attacker.

- **Be street-smart.** Ask for two room keys so it appears you're not alone. Sign the hotel register with your first initial and last name. If a stranger follows you, return to the front desk, report the incident, and ask for an escort. If you have a rental car, park under a light and look in the backseat before getting in. Pity the fool who tries to hide in your car because he'll get a stiletto stuck into his head.

- **Trust your gut.** If the guy in the elevator looks like a creep, wait for the next elevator. Don't get your exercise by taking the isolated staircase—use the hotel gym and increase your strength for self-defense.

- **Get out of the room.** Turn off the free Internet and take advantage of the local attractions. In large cities, you usually can find a single theatre ticket in orchestra seating, and the concierge can help with taxi and dinner reservations. If you forget where you're staying, you shouldn't travel.

- **Learn new technology.** I was recently on a trip that included flying out of state, renting a car, and driving in the dark. My adult children taught me how to program route instructions through Pandora on my cell phone and plug the information into my car radio. Every few miles, a gentle voice told me where to go. And I obeyed.

- **Realize that the world offers wonderful sights and adventures,** but it's also full of horrible criminals who would cut off your finger to get your diamond ring. Turn your rings around, stay alert, and arrive alive.

One last word of advice: if a slick guy at the hotel bar asks if you need a little company, just tell him you already bought one last week. Works every time.

~

It's Time to Face the Music

The small advertisement appeared as a nugget of nostalgia between the like-new drum set and the antique piano: "1970s jukebox. Works sometimes. $100 or best offer." For a brief, irrational moment, I considered buying it. Then I remembered that my smartphone contained more music than a jukebox, and it fit better in my pocket.

Jukeboxes are unwanted relics of a slower yesterday, the true Happy Days. Our generation turned out the lights on our parents' bugle boys as they wrapped stardust melodies with a string of pearls. We preferred the uncomplicated, steady beat of "Louie, Louie" and could buy it from a Wurlitzer with bubbling lights. Now the ability to instantly download any song at any time means that people miss out on the memorable magic of the jukebox experience.

I remember plunking in coins and pushing the buttons to hear songs from the 1960s. As teenagers wearing loafers and sweater sets, we eagerly watched as a vinyl record was mechanically pulled from the stack and placed on the spinning turntable. Then the needle swiveled over to latch into the groove to produce the sound. For farm kids in Wendell, this was as close as we would ever get to the live band.

On the checkered tile floors in the crowded cafés of our youth, we danced the Pony and the Twist and the Watusi as our ponytails bounced and dour chaperones scowled in disapproval from the sidelines. We never questioned the inane lyrics of "Wooly Bully" from Sam the Sham and the Pharaohs, and we wailed with Lesley Gore singing "It's My Party." Everything changed when disco assaulted our senses with mirrored balls and jerky movements. But still, we danced.

During the early 1970s, we rode in the backs of pickup trucks with the music blaring over portable radios, and we vowed to never get old. When we danced, we shouted "Hot Stuff" along with Donna Summer. Our luckier friends owned cars with 8-track tape players, and we traveled further away from our collections of scratchy vinyl records and electricity-dependent jukeboxes.

The 1980s tempered our free spirits as many of us married and had children. When we had the opportunity to dance, it was to the music of Michael Jackson's "Billie Jean" and the Eurythmics' "Sweet Dreams." The jukeboxes were relegated to collectors and antique stores, and our cars replaced 8-track players with cassette players. Those of us with small children suffered through ghastly songs from a demented dinosaur named Barney and sweet songs from Raffi until we rebelled and taught our kids classics, such as "A Horse with No Name" by America.

Dance music lost its way during the 1990s when the most popular song was the "Macarena" by Los Del Rio. It was stupid, and we refused to do it. Things didn't improve in 2000 when hip hop substituted rhythm and lyrics with noise and profanity. Yes, we were aging and becoming the old farts we used to pity. Most of us just wanted the simplicity of good dance songs, and we were sustained with ageless musicians, including Elton John, the Rolling Stones, and Tina Turner.

The husky tones of a new voice brought hope in 2010 when Adele introduced "Rolling in the Deep" and Katy Perry ignited the air with "Firework." We could dance to those songs.

We don't ride in the back of pickup trucks anymore, and we've broken our pledge to never get older. But we still refuse to be the grumpy sourpusses muttering in the corner. We want music, and we will dance. A little slower now, but we will dance.

At the risk of sounding like your indignant parents, just read the lyrics of the most popular songs. That will make you want to give away your possessions to go live in the forest and wistfully play a flute beside a mountain stream.

As a crusty, crabby but often comical curmudgeon, I regretfully lament the disappearance of quality lyrics in pop culture. With apologies to Pete Seeger's original song, I ask "Where have all the lyrics gone?" Over the past fifty years, we've gone from "I want to hold your hand" to "If I eat you like a cannibal ain't nothing to it gangsta rap made me do it."

The number-one song of 1964 was "You've Lost that Loving Feeling" by the Righteous Brothers. The opening lyrics were poignant:

You never close your eyes anymore when I kiss your lips.
And there's no tenderness like before in your fingertips.

One of the top songs today is "Drunk in Love" performed by Beyoncé Knowles. Here are some of the lyrics in her top-rated song:

We woke up in the kitchen saying,
"How in the hell did this sh#t happen?"

Nice.

And who wouldn't be inspired by the creative words of Miley Cyrus singing in her pop tune "We Can't Stop":

To my home girls here with the big butts,
shaking it like we at a strip club.

As a child star, Miley Cyrus must have missed out on English classes because she's definitely missing a verb in that sentence. And would some nice doctor please offer corrective surgery on that tongue. I've seen giraffes at the zoo with smaller tongues.

Then there's the enchanted melody of hip-hop/rap music. The 1990 song, "Fight the Power" by Public Enemy, offers this inspirational line:

I'm ready an' hyped plus I'm amped.
Most of my heroes don't appear on no stamp.

Here's the last awful lyric I can type without going blind. It's from Lady Gaga's "song" called "Beautiful, Dirty, Rich":

Beautiful and dirty dirty rich rich
we've got a redlight pornographic dance fight
systematic, honey
but we got no money.

I enjoy music that was performed from the late 1960s through the 1980s. The top ten songs from 1980 feature the works of a broad diversity of artists: Blondie, Michael Jackson, Pink Floyd, Bette Midler, Billy Joel, Queen, and Paul McCartney. I'll play their music any day. Other personal favorites include Procol Harum, Moody Blues, UB40, Carole King, and Norah Jones. I also listen to the music of current singers such as Katy Perry and Adele, and I'm a sucker for the crooners, from Frank Sinatra to Josh Groban.

But before I'm pressured to make that final decision to buy a flute and escape to the forest, I'll head down the freeway playing my favorite music. The perfect driving song is "Go West," originally by the Village People but perfected by the Pet Shop Boys. Here are some of the understandable lyrics:

Go West. Life is peaceful there. Go West. In the open air. Go West. Baby you and me. Go West. This is our destiny.

One of my New Year's resolutions was to clean out the cabinets in the garage, but I only worked fifteen minutes before I found my collection of ancient record albums. Like a giddy archeologist with an amazing discovery, I reverently opened the dusty box and gently sorted the cardboard folders. It was almost a spiritual experience when I retrieved *Meet the Beatles!* The album was released January 20, 1964— fifty years ago—and I remember.

I was just a little girl, but I'll never forget the anticipation of that first album that *Rolling Stone* magazine ranks as number 59 of the greatest 500 albums of all time. I had saved money I earned from my paper route and bought the record. I daydreamed in my bedroom as the record played on my portable player. My favorite song was "This Boy," and my favorite Beatle was Paul McCartney. I knew he was singing just for me, the gangly, frizzy-haired, glasses-wearing goofball living on an Idaho farm.

I also remember The Beatles' first appearance in the United States. It was Sunday, February 9, 1964 on the *Ed Sullivan Show*. My family always watched the show, so we crowded around our one black-and-white television set. I felt pressured to contain my excitement. I still recall Sullivan's introduction: "Ladies and gentlemen, The Beatles. Let's bring it on."

The four young men began a rousing rendition of "All My Loving," and I could tell my father was getting irritated. We begged him to listen to one more song. He relaxed when the next song was the tender "Till There Was You." But when The Beatles launched into "She Loves You," my father had heard enough. He jumped up, turned off the television, and said the noise would stop. I was crushed because I wanted to hear "I Want to Hold Your Hand." That was the final song on the show. I retreated to my bedroom and listened to the record over and over.

The Beatles were paid $10,000 for three appearances on the *Ed Sullivan Show*. That's nothing compared to the obscene amount of money wasted on some of today's mediocre performers. I predict that the current crop of crappy crooners won't be remembered five decades—or five years—from now. But somewhere a young girl will hear an original rendition of "I Saw Her Standing There," and she'll sing in her room and imagine a lover singing, "We danced through the night, and we held each other tight, and before too long

I fell in love with her. Now I'll never dance with another, since I saw her standing there."

My memory is clouded with the strains of songs that should never have been written or sung. The Captain and Tennille singing about "Muskrat Love" and The Carpenters warbling "Sing of good things, not bad. Sing of happy, not sad."

I believe those two songs were solely responsible for the rise of heavy metal bands and for Black Sabbath's song "Electric Funeral" about nuclear annihilation. It's all about balance.

To survive each New Year, I suggest that you make music an important part of your life. At the stroke of midnight on December 31, you'll take a cup of kindness yet and sing "Auld Lang Syne" with the eager passion of a professional soloist, despite knowing that when the sun rises you won't be able to carry a tune in a spiked punch bowl. But for a brief moment, when the year is new and full of untainted potential, you'll become a soulful crooner for all the ages, sharing your song with the universe.

Your challenge throughout the year is to keep the music playing. Sing and play your own songs long after the confetti is thrown into the garbage, the bills are past due, and prosperity is still elusive. The late comedian George Carlin said, "It's called The American Dream because you have to be asleep to believe it." His acerbic humor nailed it. How can you sing a joyful song when life keeps dumping junk on your head? Maybe you're unemployed or in a lousy job, or you haven't had any loving since 2008, or your dog ran away. Look on the bright side—you could write country Western songs!

Music and mood are closely related—listening to a sad or happy song alters your mood and has the ability to change your perception of the world around you. For example, gothic metal music makes me want to damage something with a chainsaw, while a classical aria causes me to (almost) levitate with elation. In a stressful situation, a little dose of "Walking on Sunshine" could be all it takes to relieve the tension.

Here are some exercises to prove that music alters your mood. Imagine seeing and hearing the following scenarios:

You're struggling in the steaming jungles of Vietnam as you hear the foreboding song "The End" by The Doors, as played in the movie *Apocalypse Now*. Then you're drinking alone in a dark bar as a Billie Holiday impersonator croons "Gloomy Sunday." You claw out of a deep depression only to hear Kansas singing "Dust in the Wind." By now you should be wallowing on the floor, sobbing in anguish about the wretched world. You're the loser in a great tragedy when you hear the music turn to the overpowering dirges reserved for horror films. It's inevitable that you'll be eaten by a Zombie just as the lady screams in the shower at the Bates Motel. The music screeches then stops.

Now, pretend you're twirling on a panoramic Austrian mountain meadow singing "The Sound of Music" with Julie Andrews. You're even wearing a summer dress with a festive apron. Then transport yourself to a sunny beach, listening to the jaunty tune of Bobby McFerrin's "Don't Worry, Be Happy." Finally, turn up the volume on "Chariots of Fire" or "Rocky." Yo, Adrian! Are you smiling yet? Sometimes I'll be driving along when a favorite tune starts to play on the radio and I'm suddenly Christmas-morning happy.

The song and the open road are there just for me and all I need to do is sing and drive with gusto and avoid speeding tickets.

No matter what festivity or calamity the next year brings, you should have a song or two ready to suit the occasion. If you can't find the perfect tune, create your own. Add it to your bucket list to make your own music by the end of the year. Don't worry if you're unsure about writing a song. Remember the immortal lyrics of that famous song that rose to #4 on the Billboard Charts—"Now he's tickling her fancy, rubbing her toes. Muzzle to muzzle, now, anything goes as they wriggle, Sue starts to giggle." That song includes synthesized sound effects simulating muskrat copulation. Yes, you can do better!

I often encourage writers to listen to various types of music to inspire their stories, poems, and journals. Occasionally I teach at local elementary schools, and I use music to encourage their busy brains to focus on writing. It's amazing to watch them seriously meditate as I play a requiem or a military march or folk song and then ask them to write down what they were envisioning as the song played. They frantically write their feelings on paper, and the brave ones stand to read. I get a bit emotional.

I also enjoy organizing writing workshops for adults. I recently hosted a women's writing retreat at my cabin in the Idaho mountains, and I was under pressure to organize the perfect experience. Just past midnight on the second night, I was working in my bedroom when the power went out. This is a normal winter occurrence, but I had guests sleeping in other bedrooms. I feared horrible calamities would result from the lack of electricity, including no morning coffee, no blow dryers, or perhaps death by freezing. All these were major problems.

I bundled up in my flannels and piled quilts on the bed, trusting that the other women would do the same. I didn't sleep much during the night because I was planning how to cope with the problem the next morning. I couldn't get my car out of the garage to go get coffee because the control on the electric garage door was too high to reach. I thought about calling a friend who owned a nearby yurt, but I didn't know if he had a generator. I worried that my paid attendees would demand a refund to pay for frostbitten fingers and toes.

Early the next morning, I took my flashlight and tiptoed out of the bedroom. That's when I saw the glowing lights from the kitchen appliances. The power was on in every room except mine. I hurried to the garage, found the correct breaker switch, flipped it back and forth, and discovered all the lights were on in my bedroom. All that worry was for nothing.

It reminded me of Glinda the Good Witch in *The Wizard of Oz* telling Dorothy, "You've always had the power, my dear. You had it all along." I plugged in the coffee pot, feeling relieved and powerful.

Being without electricity makes it tempting to throw away all electronic devices and go live in a cave. A nagging voice in our mind instigates the rebellion by sporadically echoing through the cobwebs in my middle-aged brain and whispering, "They're all out to destroy you. Run away now."

My current wave of frustration was caused by a few exasperating problems: my credit card number was fraudulently taken and used to purchase sports equipment in Delaware and a tourist trip to Australia. Then my cell phone died. Then my computer got a virus and went black while I was working on an important project. If I lived in a cave, I'd never experience these annoyances.

It took several days to deal with the issues. My computer returned from the repair shop with a perfect screen and a hefty repair bill. The credit card company canceled the card and the debts, and my cell phone just needed to be recycled. A ten-year-old child could have handled all these problems while simultaneously creating a video and texting one hundred of her closest friends.

It's a challenge to keep up with technology, especially because I grew up thinking a keyboard was on a piano, a ram was in the pasture, a cookie was something to eat, and the one telephone in the house was attached to the wall. I wrote papers and short stories on a manual typewriter and was positively giddy to get an IBM Selectric typewriter. Now I take my iPad on vacation and input, format, copy, and insert my blog with attached pictures onto the World Wide Web. Amazing.

All this marvelous technology that allows me to instantly research facts, pay bills online, book a flight, and watch a video on my cell phone also attracts evil scoundrels who steal credit card numbers and send malicious viruses through the Internet. The answer is to spend more time with my small grandchildren. They know how to download an app for that.

∿

When It's Party Time
at the Empty Nest

My middle-aged friends no longer need to worry that their daughters will bring home itinerant carnival workers who want to camp in the yard and plant marijuana in the flower beds or that their sons will grow old in the basement playing video games with their illiterate buddies. No, somehow we survived the great unknown between "You can't tell me what to do!" and "Thanks, Mom, I love you!" After decades of raising children and preparing them for the realities of the world, most women are jubilant when their young adults are without a criminal record, gainfully employed, and off of the family nickel or teat. For us, the empty nest is a positive experience because our children are doing fine on their own.

"My son got a job and has a new apartment!" Cheers and toasts.

"My daughter is starting her own business and already has a few clients." More cheers and clinking of glasses.

"My children pooled some of the money they earned and bought me a present!" Loud clapping and more drink orders.

"I've turned the empty bedroom into a wine bar and writing studio!" Total adulation and drinks for the entire bar!

Of course, we'd like to assume that the successes of our children are due to our superior parenting skills, but we're also wise enough to know that a tremendous amount of luck, blessings, and other nurturing adults were involved to help Junior and Sis become productive adults. And we've shared countless tears with good mothers struggling with their children's drug addictions, chronic unemployment, physical and mental limitations, or abusive partners. We're also keenly aware that the dismal job market makes it difficult for our eager offspring to find good employment. That's why it's so exhilarating to celebrate when our young adult sons and daughters become self-sufficient.

The rites of passage continue to evolve, and I try to anticipate the next opportunity that will tug at my heart, or bewilder my brain, or make me load my gun. Midlife brings those complex days when I rock a grandchild to sleep, exercise with my grown daughter, share a beer with my son-in-law, listen as my son describes his tough job, take a sad friend to lunch, feel my daughter-in-law's pregnant belly (but not in a creepy way), send a steamy text to my sweetheart, write a sassy short story, and then go help my ailing mother at the assisted living facility. Really, I can't imagine life any other way.

It took an empty dinner plate to make me comprehend the emotional consequences of my empty nest. I held the bright red "You Are Special Today" plate, and tears rolled down my cheeks as I realized that my children had actually followed my advice to test their wings and that there was no one at home to need the plate. For over twenty years, the red plate was used to celebrate my children's birthdays. Each birthday breakfast, they were served custom pancakes on the special plate. I made their initials in the pan and transferred the cakes to the plate, even when they were in high school. (Making an A was definitely easier than making an E.) On the evening of their birthday, dinner was a celebration as they enjoyed their favorite meal on the unique platter.

During my daughter's volatile vegetarian years, the plate was heaped with cheese lasagna and buttered corn, unless she gave herself special dispensation to have pepperoni pizza or a burger. When my son played high school football, the plate disappeared under a sizzling porterhouse steak. As they cleaned up every bite, they were rewarded with the familiar words telling them that they were, indeed, special that day. Then the plate was stored on the shelf until the next birthday.

Now the plate of platitudes wasn't needed anymore. My daughter had moved to Maui after college graduation and was working three jobs in order to cover her expenses. My son had joined the army and was serving as a military policeman in South Korea. My kids not only left the nest, they left the mainland! I was lucky to see them once or twice a year. I admonished myself for inspiring them to be so independent. While my friends lamented that their twenty-something children had moved back home or, worse yet, had never left, I sulked with sadness at their great fortune. My children were several time zones away. What did I do wrong?

The first Christmas without them was a total disaster, and I forced myself to decorate the tree and hang their favorite ornaments. During our holiday telephone conversations, I tried to sound cheerful and supportive, but after hanging up, I scurried about in a desperate search for chocolate or wine, or both, to soothe my loneliness. Ultimately, I was a mess.

After doing some research on the empty nest syndrome, I was relieved to find I wasn't alone in my sadness. Many people experience feelings of depression or grief after their children come of age and move out or go away to college. Women usually have a more difficult time than men, mainly because they have spent more time with their children. The women also could be going through menopause, which has its own set of emotional issues that are exacerbated by an empty nest. The problems are compounded when women experience physical problems associated with getting older or if they're caring for aging parents. To hell with being called the sandwich generation. We're the sack lunch of left-over stale chips. Our energy is depleted and we need chocolate now if we're ever going to survive this woeful reality.

After I grew tired of feeling sorry for myself, I decided to turn my sadness into positive energy. I saved money and took a trip to Maui to spend time with my daughter. I had no desire to visit South Korea, so I sent goofy cards and humorous gifts to my son and waited eagerly for his monthly telephone calls. My son was in South Korea for two holiday seasons, and our family used the experience to concentrate less on the material craziness associated with the season and to focus more on the meaning of family and freedom. It was truly cathartic when I reached for the "You Are Special Today" plate and used it myself for New Year's Day dinner. It was the beginning of a new life for me.

In hindsight, I was totally unprepared for the truth. I will live without my children much longer than I lived with them. That's a difficult reality after submerging twenty years of my life into the responsibilities, joys, and frustrations of raising kids. Now that they're happy, productive adults, I can look back at those years as a brief, marvelous moment in time when I received the "special plate" every day because I had the privilege to be their mother. If you're in the same precarious predicament, here are some suggestions to cope with the empty nest syndrome.

- **Remember the Song "Cat's in the Cradle."** Yes, the lyrics from the song by Harry Chapin are true. We're so busy when our children are young that we forget that they'll be grown up and gone in the blink of an eye. Take time to savor the years with your children. Besides, you need to keep a good relationship with your kids because you'll need their assistance when you're old and feeble. Pretend you have millions of dollars stashed away so they'll be sure to visit often and bring treats.

- **Prepare for Parting.** If your child is getting ready to leave for college, plan for a family vacation or adventure before he or she leaves home. Celebrate the future and provide encouragement because your child may be just as apprehensive as you are. However, don't feel too bad if he or she runs out the door shouting, "Alleluia!" That just means you've given them some powerful and positive wings with which to fly. But if they don't seem appreciative of all you did for them, move away and don't share your forwarding address.

- **Give Them the True Gifts.** Your children should leave home with the ability to survive. They need to know how to do laundry, balance a checkbook, cook a meal, and get a job. They also need to know that they'll always be welcomed home any time with open arms, a clean bed, and a warm meal waiting for them. And if you've taught them well, they'll come home and do your laundry, cook the meals, and clean up the mess. That's a successful parent!

- **Reorganize Your Life.** It's all different now and will never be the same. You need to assess your personal transition from primary caregiver to part-time peer. Your children want you to be happy, and they don't need any guilt trips on their journey to independence. You can have the same feeling of freedom that they have if you're willing to explore your own potential. And no, you can't move into their dorm room and be best friends.

- **Don't Start "Pre-Grieving."** There's an online website that actually has links to regular blogs for people who are "pre-grieving." Even though their children are still at home, the parents already have begun to lament the time when their kids will leave home. With all due respect, it's time to get a grip and a life. I know middle-aged people whose grown children are still living with them. Don't be that parent.

- **Relish Your Relationships.** If you're married, you now have an opportunity to rekindle the dormant passion that was put on the back burner while you dedicated your time to raising children. You may have to dig out the old photos, songs, and costumes to remind you of a friskier time. If you're single, find some groups that cater to single men and women. You don't have to rush into a serious relationship, but it's nice to have a friend to share dinner and a movie. Beware of jerks who prowl online dating sites and brag about their money, achievements, dashing good looks, and prowess in the bedroom. If all that were true, they wouldn't need a dating service.

- **Related Resources.** You can find information to assist with your transition from full house to empty nest. Check online for relevant books, organizations, articles, message boards, events, and services. Remember that you're not the first person to experience an empty nest. And you won't be the last. Enjoy the free time before your kids send you to a nursing home.

After my children left home, I experienced several episodes of total anguish because I missed the commotion of children in the house. There were dreary times that could only be cured by a container of butter pecan ice cream. But now, in the glorious goodness of life, both my children have moved closer to my home. And I am enjoying a true blessing of being this darned old because now grandchildren are planting sticky kisses on my cheek.

It's fun to tell my grandchildren about favorite times when their parents were young. When my kids were three and five, we took them to Disneyland because we wanted to spend our life's savings to stand in line with a million sweaty people and wait an hour for a thirty-second ride. Disneyland was celebrating Donald Duck's fiftieth birthday, and the speech-impaired duck was my three-year-old son's favorite funny character (besides me, of course). Wishing for a cattle prod, we maneuvered our way to the front of the crowd for the afternoon Magic Kingdom Parade and waited eagerly to be enchanted. On days when I border on madness (too numerous to count), I can still hear the cacophony of the calliope as the giant duck sang, "It's Donald's birthday, it's Donald's birthday!"

After the parade ended, my usually-ebullient son began sobbing uncontrollably. I asked what was wrong, and he answered, "Because it's over." At that moment, I would have given everything I owned to make the parade start again, but I knew that was impossible (I didn't own that much), so I sat on the curb and held him until he stopped crying. What else do you do when the magic goes away?

Most of us have seen several decades of parades, and sometimes we feel deflated when the commotion stops. We go from the season of high school and college graduations to all the summer weddings. Each celebration deserves elaborate fanfare, but we know from experience that the festivities come to an end. That's when new graduates realize they must (pick at least one):

- Get a job
- Marry rich
- Move out of their parents' basement
- Invent a better Facebook-Video Game-Vibrator (Hmm, not a bad idea…)

And the newlyweds realize their spouse (pick at least one):

- Farts on the hour and belches sulfur
- Cries about road kill
- Faints at your kid's projectile vomiting
- Gets diarrhea at dinner parties

Then your new spouse gets dramatically alarmed when you sleep with a:

- Humming teddy bear

- Dog

- Nasty magazine

- Picture of mother

Yes, that's when the parade is over, and there's not a damn thing we can do about it. We just need to hold ourselves until we stop crying.

Many middle-aged women experience empty nest syndrome after the youngest child leaves home for college, jail, the circus, or to find him/herself. After at least eighteen years of majestically sacrificing our lives for our delightful offspring, they gleefully run out the door and into the dangerous world without a helmet or a clean change of underwear. Our tears stop when they turn around to come back, but it's only to ask for gas money. We slink back to our reruns of the *Carol Burnett Show* and pathetically relate to the cleaning lady at the end who sweeps up the mess and turns off the lights.

Good news! Now is your opportunity to turn that empty bedroom into a retreat for:

- Sewing, craft, and writing projects

- A private wine bar

- Afternoon sex

- Séances with Madam Moonbeam (great write-off)

- All of the above

Do it now so the kids can't move back and bring their pet spider collection, garage band, and/or online gambling addiction. Also, you could use your extra time to take a class, try yoga, volunteer, or start a creative project. You may want to focus on your physical and mental health; maybe talk to a professional about that stupid duck song that keeps squawking in your head. Or (my favorite suggestion) become the drum major of your own parade; just don't forget to tip the guy who cleans up after the horses. And, of course, any midlife parade is best enjoyed with a bold red wine.

After the last kid grows up and flies down the road to chart his or her own path, get ready for a new adventure: you have more time, the house is quiet, and you don't have to hide your favorite ice cream behind the frozen ham hocks anymore.

∼

Adventures in Eldercare

I recently visited my mother in her assisted living facility, and she was sitting in her wheelchair looking at a copy of *ESPN* magazine.

"Studying for the Super Bowl?" I asked.

"No," she responded. "I don't like sports."

I noticed the stack of magazines on her table. *Forbes. Men's Health. Ebony. Jet. Yoga Today. Elle.*

"Have you been taking your medications, Mom?" I asked, wondering about her sudden interest in all things young and masculine.

"I don't like those magazines," she answered. "I'm waiting for my prize."

She wheeled over to her dresser and pulled out a large envelope stuffed with "official" letters and postcards from the Office of the Senior Vice President of Publishers Clearing House announcing that she was in the Winners Circle! Yes, she only had a limited time to return the card with the Official Authorization Code to be eligible to collect her millions in prizes! But the time-sensitive message was urgent! "The next step is up to you!" screamed the bold text highlighted in bright yellow. "You could be just days away from winning! Respond today!" And, of course, it wouldn't hurt to subscribe to some of these magazines…

My mother had dutifully written notes on each and every letter: day received, amount of check enclosed, day check mailed. She already had subscribed to most of the women's magazines, including *Cooking* (she doesn't have a kitchen) and *Oprah* (empowerment has never been part of her lifestyle). I tallied up the orders, and she had paid for thirty-two magazine subscriptions, some of them until 2016. And there was no Prize Patrol pounding on her door.

My mother is not stupid, just frail. She's a Depression-era woman who knows the value of a penny, and thirty years ago she helped my father manage several large businesses. In her defense, I know that she grew up in a time when women took oaths to "obey," and they believed every official-looking document they received. The evil hucksters at PCS know how to manipulate these innocent people, but the fraud they're committing against the elderly should be labeled a criminal offense.

I made a note to get the subscriptions cancelled, but I suspected that would be almost as difficult as winning anything. I also considered staging an event to have some people show up at her door with balloons and a big (worthless) check. I really want her to get a prize.

As we stacked the magazines, I felt her slip into a depression. It was time to call out the clowns.

"Hey Mom, you'll never guess what the grandkids did last week!"

She perked up and waited for the story. I scrambled to think of something funny.

"Well, we were making cookies and Sweetie Pie stuffed some of the batter up her nose!"

Mom smiled so I continued.

"And Pumpkin laughed so hard she wet her pants."

Mom giggled and then said, "Well, I do that all the time."

We laughed and for a second I saw the old sparkle return to her eyes. Then she turned to the labeled photos on the wall.

"Which one is Pumpkin?" she asked.

I pointed to her great-granddaughter.

"Oh, yes," she said. "I remember her."

Mom's dementia fades in and out. Most of the time she remembers me, but sometimes she'll look at me with confusion as if I'm a long-lost friend who came to visit.

"I want to walk again," she said.

"I know. But you've had a broken hip and a broken back. And remember all the physical therapists we saw? They worked to get you walking, but then there were other falls. I think the wheelchair is safe for now."

She nodded in resignation. "At least the chair is closer to the floor when I fall out of it."

I smiled and reached for her shawl. "Let's go outside for some fresh air."

I pushed her chair down the hall and outside onto the porch. We stopped in a sunny spot and I pulled up a chair. We watched traffic go up and down the main street of town, and she seemed content.

"Is it Christmas yet?" she asked.

"No, not for a few months," I answered.

"You know, I was a child during the Great Depression. For Christmas I got a fresh orange in a pair of new wool stockings. But before I could open my present, I had to milk the cows by hand in the barn and feed the horses."

"I grumble if I have to make my bed before opening presents," I said. I wished that life had been easier for her.

"I have a busy week coming up. I get my hair done on Wednesday and I have two showers this week."

"Well aren't you the busy one?" I replied.

She got quiet and I feared she would go back into a depression.

"I hope Elaine will visit soon. She's my daughter."

"I'm sure she'll be here," I said while I silently cursed the dementia.

"I want my car," she said.

"Well, Mom, do you remember when you drove your car through the back of your garage panicked, shoved the gear into reverse, and then smashed into the closing garage door? You had two dented fenders, a hole in the wall, a broken garage door, and a wounded ego. Your car resembled the winning entry in a demolition derby from all the dings and dents. Fortunately for everyone, they weren't caused by running over a kid on a bicycle."

She stared at me. "I never ran over any kid!"

"I know, Mom. I was just teasing. But the car was damaged so I had to take it to the repair shop. We're still waiting for parts."

I didn't tell her that I sold her car four years ago but I refused to drive on a guilt trip. I know that a car is the last symbol of independence, and I'll hide the keys if anyone ever comes for mine.

"Besides, I don't think you want to drive anywhere. The roads are terrible this time of year."

She nodded in agreement and then shivered. We rolled back into her room and I hung up her shawl. Then I noticed a scratch in her cedar chest.

"How did that happen, Mom?"

"Oh, my wheelchair ran into it when I wasn't looking."

That seemed like a perfectly logical response. My mother received the cedar chest as a present from her parents when she graduated from Wendell High School in 1945. Back then, young women prepared for their future home long before they were married. They sewed pillowcases, knitted blankets, and collected linens to store in the trunk. My mom, the timid valedictorian, was engaged to my father, the popular student body president. Her cedar-lined hope chest symbolized an escape from her life of farm work.

I opened the chest and sorted the contents that had given her such hope over the years: her wedding dress in a clouded dress bag, unused satin pillowcases turned yellow with age, a pink blanket still waiting to swaddle two baby girls who never breathed, old newspapers, a folder of Paul Harvey columns, letters from my father when he served overseas in the military, a gold locket, faded photographs of nameless people, a portrait of my father—so handsome at eighteen before myriad illnesses and a lifetime of stress ravaged his body.

Mom watched as I carefully repacked the chest and closed the lid.

"I think we should let everything rest and go to lunch," she said.

We enjoyed a bland, soft-food lunch in the pleasant dining room along with forty other residents. During the meal, she dumped her water glass into the vase of plastic flowers on the table, explaining that the blossoms lasted longer that way. I nodded in agreement.

I've finally learned to accept such actions. Over the past few years, it's been a struggle for me to acknowledge her mental deterioration. There has been a cadre of physical therapists to keep her active, various puzzles and workbooks to challenge her brain, and regular family activities with the grandchildren and their children. Despite our best efforts, she is slipping away.

We took dessert back to her room because it was time for reruns of *The Lawrence Welk Show* and it was "vunderful, vunderful." The two of us feasted on chocolate fudge cake with ice cream as we watched the show. Oh yes, Mr. Welk appeared splendid in his canary-yellow suit, and the orchestra looked so festive in traffic-cone orange. Two dancers from the audience were dressed in identical orange and lime-green outfits. We named every performer, and in moments of poignant reality, Mom could identify which ones had died. And she was amazed that Mr. Welk still looked so young.

I used to love the live *Lawrence Welk Show*. It was right up there with *Bonanza, The Carol Burnett Show,* and *I Love Lucy.* I had paper dolls of the Lennon Sisters—Diane, Kathy, Peggy, and Janet. The Christmas shows were delightful, as the performers brought their children for the gift exchange. Watching the show was a Saturday night ritual. I don't know what my daughter and I will be watching twenty years from now, but there is a high possibility that we'll be sharing chocolate fudge cake with ice cream.

The worst part of watching television with my mother was watching her try to manipulate the controls. I tried many times to teach her how to use the television remote control but finally gave up.

"I can't do it!" she cried.

Not even her love of *The Lawrence Welk Show* could motivate her to remember how to push the power button and then the correct channel button. So I stopped trying, and we're both happier. I requested that the patient, loving staff now assist her on Saturday nights at 7:00 p.m. to turn on the television. My unspoken fear is that I may duplicate the scene with my children, but we'll wait to face that drama.

While she watched the rest of the show, I visited the doctor. We discussed Mom's prognosis and treatment.

"Do you still carry the DNR file?" he asked. I nodded yes.

He was referring to the Do Not Resuscitate file, a folder I automatically grab if the telephone rings at an unusual time. The call comes at any hour: "Your mother is in an ambulance on the way to the hospital." I grab the DNR file and go, anticipating that she will survive the latest calamity just as she has for the past eighty-six years. Her mind and body are frail, but her heart is strong, and her determination to live should be studied for medical research because she'll outlive all of us.

Only caregivers of invalid parents can understand the experience of being the keeper of the DNR file, a responsibility I willing, respectfully accepted twenty-four years ago. But sometimes, when I'm speeding away with The File, I yell at the universe because she has suffered too much and I can't do anything except carry the instructions that prove she has chosen Do Not Resuscitate.

If you're designated as the keeper of the DNR file, that means you're probably the only daughter. Somehow sons aren't willing or able to assume the responsibilities. Here is what you'll need:

1. A POST Document—Physician Orders for Scope of Treatment—outlines what lifesaving procedures the patient wants. The form is signed in advance by the patient and a doctor and includes choices from Allow Natural Death to Use Aggressive Intervention. There should be an additional category for Survivors of the Great Depression. These people redefine the human capacity for survival.

2. A copy of the Living Will designating you as the Power of Attorney over Health Care. This role can lead you to drink. More.

3. A photo identification of the patient. My mother no longer drives, but you can get a non-driver, photo ID at the Department of Motor Vehicles. If you have any problems at the DMV, just threaten to leave your mother sitting there in her wheelchair and walk away. Works every time.

4. A detailed inventory of all medications, including doses. This list will cause you to throw down your plate of maple bars and enroll in multiple exercise programs while you still have time.

5. Copies of health insurance information including Social Security number, Medicaid number, and any supplemental insurance details. Then toss in some medications (chocolate, vodka) for yourself because it can be a bumpy ride.

For my mother's DNR file, I also include some spiritual music because she likes it and because it keeps me from dissolving into a puddle of mush when she revives and doesn't know who I am or why I'm there. That's when I pray for an extra jolt of my mother's tenacity for me because I'm dangerously close to jumping out of the hospital's top-floor window.

I talked with the doctor about my mother's recent stroke.

"She was in the hospital and the staff said she was in critical condition," I reminded him. "She got all the way to POST Section C: No Feeding tube. No IV fluid. No Antibiotics. The hospice staff told me she had seventy-two hours to live and to make funeral arrangements, so I did."

I described going to the funeral home, meeting with the soft-spoken funeral director, choosing the casket, and discussing costs. Then I returned to the hospital to wait in Mom's room and play music and read to her. After fifty hours without food or water, she opened her eyes and said, "Hi!"

"Doctor, I don't want to go through that experience again," I said.

He agreed. "She's one tough lady," was all he could say.

Over the past sixteen years, there have been serious car accidents, a broken back, a broken hip and other broken bones, severe falls that resulted in concussions, numerous bruises, stitches, slurring of words, and bouts of pneumonia, dementia issues, and several stays in various rehabilitation facilities. It truly breaks my heart to see her in these situations, and all I can do is hold her hand, play music, read to her, and just be there. Several times the medical staff has counseled me in hushed tones that she wouldn't live. I usually chuckle and say, "Just watch."

After meeting with the doctor, I returned to Mom's room and found her asleep in her chair. I turned off the television and gathered my purse and the unread magazines and started to leave.

"I want my car," she woke and said.

"Still waiting for parts," I replied.

We shook our heads and muttered in mutual disbelief. Then she went back to sleep. For now, I'll continue to make the 250-mile roundtrip journey to Wendell, my hometown, to make small talk with my mother. And we will continue to water the artificial flowers.

∼

Grandkids as Speed Bumps

Suddenly I'm on the other side of fifty, my grown children are telling me how to drive, and a cute little squirt is calling me grandma. How did this happen? What should I do about it? I need some chocolate. But the grandkids are growing on me.

After my daughter had her first baby I call Pumpkin, we shared a Quintessa cabernet. It was a sobering decision to choose between wine and a week's groceries, but the special occasion called for a superior wine. And continuing my valuable bloodline certainly is cause for jubilation and excessive merriment! While the perfect little cherub nestled in her handmade basket, swaddled in an organic blanket, her proud parents and I toasted her birth and savored our way through the Quintessa.

A few years later, when my splendid son and delightful daughter-in-law announced that they were expecting a baby, I began the necessary arrangements by sampling wines to commemorate the grand birthday. I believe that sipping and sharing an exquisite wine is a better tribute than shooting bullets into the sky, or organizing a regional festival complete with marching bands and roasted pigs, or renting those obnoxious jumping castles that could collapse or float away in a strong wind.

The miracle of birth never ceases to amaze me, and I'm grateful that I have the opportunity to see my delightful children and their charming spouses as new parents. That's one of the many positive features about getting older. I'll be there to help when needed, to bite my tongue at every tantrum, and loudly praise every piece of colorful artwork taped onto the refrigerator. And I'll spoil my grandkids to my heart's content. This grandparent gig is a lot of fun.

Three decades ago, the labor and delivery process was a lonely experience for me. I always wanted to have a waiting room full of eager relatives, similar to the scene in *Father of the Bride II,* and that's what we shared when my son's baby was born. The baby's grandparents, aunt, uncle, and cousins gathered for the grand announcement, and there was a nervous energy until my son appeared and tried to be cool and calm—except he was trembling with joy. I shed a tear because my baby just had a baby, and the world became a better place. Until that day, October 2 had been an ordinary day on the calendar. Now it is forever recognized as Baby Boo's birthday, and we'll celebrate the date every year with parties, cakes, and an assortment of fine wines.

So much has changed since my son was born thirty years ago, and technology has enhanced the labor and delivery scene for the entire family. Throughout her day in labor, my daughter-in-law sent text messages:

11:57 am – Contractions every 2-3 minutes.
12:54 pm – Dilated 4 cm.

3:36 pm – Dilated 5 cm.
5:20 pm – Holy Cow! I'm at 10!

Baby Boo arrived at 6:00 p.m., and by 6:30 we were all in the room and I had taken a photo with my cell phone and posted it on the Internet through Facebook. Within eighteen hours, the baby had been professionally photographed, and a digital version was available for purchase. That little girl came into a world of tremendous advances and incredible inventions, and we'll all watch her journey with amazement.

The mad chaos of the world seems to diminish when we're handed a newborn baby snuggly swaddled up to her chubby cheeks and button nose.

Soon after Baby Boo was born, we honored the blessed event with a red wine from Dunham Cellars in Columbia Valley, Washington. It was grand fun to raise my waiting glass and hear the familiar clinks, knowing that the future will bring laughter, more celebrations, and another bundle of wonder crawling onto my lap and saying, "Tell me another story, Tutu."

As we celebrated, someone mentioned a recent study that stated wine was worse for the brain than beer. After considerable pawing through various magazines, they retrieved the unbelievable article and displayed the alarming news:

"Too much wine damages the brain more than beer or spirits, scientists have discovered. New research on the long-term effects of heavy drinking shows that one area of the brains of wine drinkers was smaller than that of other people studied who drank different drinks in greater amounts. The ground-breaking study shows that the hippo-campus, the part of the brain involved in memory, spatial tasks and many other functions, was more than 10 percent smaller in those whose favorite drink was wine than in those who favored beer."

As a result of this information, I made an important decision: stop reading articles like this.

Watching my grandchildren can be therapeutic. My little granddaughter cries for three main reasons: she's hungry, she's tired, or her diapers are dirty. I don't need to be changed, but I could really use a sandwich and a nap. Maybe if I cry out loud...

I was raised to be tough, and crying wasn't allowed in my childhood home on the farm. That's why, as an adult, I never shed a tear while giving birth to an eleven-pound baby or while speaking at my father's funeral. But lately, I start weeping at the simple vision of a rainbow or the sound of a children's choir. And a sappy television commercial can send me over the edge into my own private pity pool.

Blame it on menopausal hormones combined with the emotions of being old enough to receive AARP mailings, but I'm not sure how to handle this new fluctuation between Iron Woman and Middle-Age Milquetoast. The recent death of a dear friend exacerbates the mental upheaval because I'm still mad that she's gone while there are so many healthy jerks walking around annoying people. She was the Dragon Slayer, but she lost the final battle to breast cancer.

I've been known to walk out of movies that portray women as weak tools or to throw down books, such as the bestseller *Eat, Pray, Love,* that insult my female warrior. The author describes lying on the floor sobbing in a fetal position. For crying out loud, she was in Italy! Get up, go outside, visit a museum, light a candle in a cathedral, or find a quaint sidewalk café and have some crusty bread, soft cheese, green olives, and red wine. If you really need a reason to wallow in pity, try growing up on a pig farm in southern Idaho!

Here is an important caveat: I realize that depression, mental illness, and anxiety attacks are serious issues, and I don't mock those who suffer from those afflictions. I advocate treatment, counseling, and a lifetime focus on healing for those who suffer from depression. For the rest of us, it's okay to experience the occasional meltdown and unleash the tears. After all, research indicates that emotional tears contain beta-endorphins that make us feel better and are a natural way to relieve mental and physical pain. So let those tears flow and wash out the toxins and stress. Then blow your nose, run outside, and play with gusto as you slay some dragons.

Margaret Crepeau, PhD, professor of nursing at Marquette University, believes that healthy people view tears positively, while people plagued with various illnesses see them as unnecessary and humiliating. She notes that well men and women cry more tears more often than women and men with ulcers and colitis. At Marquette's School of Nursing, students and professionals are urged to avoid tranquilizers and to allow tears to do their own therapeutic work. My advice to young women is: Listen to your body; it's saying, "Stop biting my lip and just enjoy a good cry!"

After several decades of eating nails for a snack, I've decided to change the menu. I'm tired of being brave all the time, so I'm choosing to put down the sword and pick up a glass of wine. I'll be tough again tomorrow. Maybe, as a true test, tonight I'll watch the illustrious Bette Midler in the movie *Beaches*. Where are those tissues?

Here's a poignant example of another important lesson I've learned from my grandchildren. I'm usually running out of the door while texting and juggling a loaded alligator bag the size of a real alligator. When I leave on a relaxing vacation, I take a laptop computer, an iPad, and a cell phone and all the necessary electronic chargers that are more important than a change of underwear. I'm often so distracted that I haven't noticed that it's not July anymore.

But a recent event caused me to (temporarily) pull the multiple plugs on my electronic taskmasters. My first clue that I was living life in a self-imposed blender was when I realized the hairs on my chin were long enough to braid because I hadn't found the time to pluck them.

I couldn't go an hour without checking in on the various email and social media sites, sometimes at stoplights. I desperately needed therapy, and I found the perfect distraction. I unplugged with the help of a fifty-pound, six-year-old speed bump: my darling granddaughter, Pumpkin.

Pumpkin and I were dashing about on one of our play dates when she stopped short, put her hands on her hips, and loudly proclaimed: "Tutu. Slow down!"

And so I did.

I looked at this darling little wonder who all too soon would be off to explore the world and not have time for a disheveled grandmother. Then I turned off the cell phone and announced that we were off the clock. Suddenly, the pace was less frantic, and my eye stopped twitching.

We were close to a craft store so decided to go inside and explore. Pumpkin wanted to create a flower arrangement for her mother, my daughter. I watched as she took thirty minutes to select the flowers, a purple vase, put back the flowers and select different flowers, choose just the right ribbon, return and pick her original selection of flowers, and arrange them gently in the order of the colors in a rainbow. Finally, she was satisfied with her creation.

By then, I was about to suggest that we just get a generic gift card, but I noticed her happy expression as she clutched her creative mommy bouquet. This delightful speed bump caused me to slow down, and I'm grateful.

I survived many decades without a computer, cell phone, or iPad. My new goal is to limit their use to a few hours in the morning, unless I'm writing. My fifty-pound therapist taught me that it's time to unplug and hug.

Besides being an excellent speed bump, small grandchildren also can assist with physical fitness and diet. Chase one around for a few days, and you'll find out why.

My new Toddler Diet has been successful in making me more fit due to increased physical activity, regular weight-lifting, and healthy eating. My toddler granddaughter visited overnight and we had a lovely time reading books, playing with toys, hiding in the pantry, scampering up and down stairs, dancing to music, and sharing exquisite snacks of banana puffs, cheese, apple sauce, and turkey sandwiches, topped off with some warm organic milk. There was no time for my usual staples of chocolate and red wine. Besides, her parents left explicit instructions that she could have no wine.

A local toy store recently went out of business, so I stocked up enough supplies to open a professional childcare facility. I estimate that I've reduced my waist two inches by picking up those toys one million times. I'm finally getting smarter at this grandmother thing and have stored most of the toys in plastic boxes. (I got the boxes to organize my office, but that's another issue.) I also lifted the twenty-five-pound darling enough times to know that's the amount of weight I need to lose so I can continue to scamper up and down stairs. She makes me laugh with her energy and antics, and when she's drifting off to sleep, she makes me cry. If I have to be this old, I might as well enjoy some sweet time rocking a baby.

Our generation has redefined the term grandmother. My grandmothers were the quintessential matrons: they grew lush gardens, baked pies, canned peaches, crocheted doilies, and then peacefully passed away in their nineties. My life has been a bit different, and I just hope I don't die tomorrow by getting hit by a wine truck while dancing in the street on my way to a comedy club. Of course, there will be a designated driver but it won't be me.

My paternal grandmother never owned a driver's license because she never needed to go anywhere. She could walk to the grocery store and post office, and she was content to sit in her rocking chair in her tidy little house. She finished crossword puzzles every day, read her Bible, and believed her life was blessed beyond measure. She was correct.

My maternal grandmother sewed dolls and grew glorious gladiolus to enter in the Jerome County Fair. She stored the numerous winning ribbons in a shoe box because she was humble, quiet, and unpretentious. Only after her death did I learn that all she wanted in life was to own a piano. I wish I could have given one to her.

Their tough example gave me a strong foundation that sustained me during the numerous personal calamities and monstrous mistakes in my life. They would be disappointed in my failures, but they would be proud of me for having the courage to be independent and tenacious. I can hear them saying, "You can do it. Now get to work."

I look at my granddaughters with wonder and worry. What will their future hold? Can they travel the world, employ their talents, and be strong in relationships? Will they treasure the self-sufficient strength of their great-great-grandmothers? Will they be able to grow a garden, bake a pie, preserve peaches, and crochet doilies? Okay, no one needs doilies anymore, but the other skills are important.

I hope they can learn from this weathered Tutu that they also can have a job, chart their own path, own a business, and challenge the boundaries. They can go beyond my grandmothers' wildest dreams, and I am confident they will likely go beyond my dreams, accomplishing things I can't even imagine. I relish their feisty and vibrant spirit. I imagine the day when they get married and then bring me a laughing baby to rock. I think Great Tutu will be a fitting name.

I adore my little granddaughters, and we laugh together as we sing and tell great stories. I am not that adept at canning fruits and vegetables, but I can encourage them to take the path less traveled, color outside the lines, and question authority. They come from a strong heritage of tough women, and I know my grandmothers are watching over them, whispering, "You can do it. Now get to work."

Sometimes we need to remember how to survive a grandchild sleepover without needing a manual or medication. When my charming granddaughter Sweetie Pie is finished with her meal, she throws the dishes and leftover food from her highchair tray onto the floor, crosses her arms, and smiles at me. I tried this once in a restaurant and was asked to leave.

At least I don't need to guess what Sweetie Pie wants. Milk? Yes! Book? Yes! Nap? No! Adult life should be so simple. Can you imagine pointing to a bottle of wine, pounding your hand on the table, and expecting someone to jump up and bring a full glass along with a plate of imported cheese, Italian olives, and crusty bread? No, me neither.

I recently experienced a four-night sleepover with three-year-old Sweetie Pie. She loves cheese, strawberries, books, and being rocked while I sing to her. The only thing she doesn't like is when I try to fix her hair. We've settled on three misaligned pigtails.

It's a mixture of fun and exhaustion when a grandchild stays overnight, so here are my suggestions for surviving the slumber party:

- Smile politely when your grown child hands you a baby with a two-page list of instructions because somehow they forgot that you raised them without a manual or explanatory DVD.

- Note how your hearing improves significantly during the night because any cough or whimper shocks you wide awake to scurry to their room to make sure they're still breathing.

- Remember that crayons will stain the grout in your expensive travertine floor, but you don't want to stifle a budding artist.

- Child-proof the kitchen: use bungee cords to secure the cabinet drawers, and lock up the booze or you'll be guzzling gin by noon. Stock at least one shelf with plastic bowls for them to pull out and throw around. You'll get plenty of exercise picking up everything.

- Know that your spouse will magically disappear when it's time to change diapers but instantly return when you and your precious little chef are making chocolate chip cookies.

- Never tell the parents that you and their organic child stayed up late to share ice cream and cookies while watching *Blazing Saddles*.

- Relish the moment when your grandchildren want to give you one more hug when it's time to go home. Assure them they can return as soon as your eye stops twitching.

- Momentarily appreciate how quiet the house is after they leave. Then plan for the next visit. This is your legacy we're talking about.

One of the many interesting facts about Sweetie Pie is that she has Down syndrome. She is a reminder that blessings can come in small, unpredictable packages that may not look like or learn as quickly as others. She is a radiant example of abundant and unconditional love in a world too focused on perfect images and shallow affection. I've learned a lot from Sweetie Pie, and I look forward to her next visit.

When my fabulous granddaughter was a toddler, her parents allowed her to come over for a play date with me at least one day a week. On a recent visit, I had to run some errands, so she agreed to come with me. That was mainly because I secured her in the car seat, and she had no choice.

I hauled her into the bank where all work stopped so the tellers could make goo-goo sounds at her. Then we went to the store and bought some disposable diapers. Her mommy wore cloth diapers when she was a baby, and I must admit these disposable things are a lot more efficient.

Then we stopped by Seasons Bistro because I had to finalize arrangements for a donation to the local charity gala. Well, of course they made me sample a tiny taste of wine that would be offered at the event. How could I refuse?

So, there I was with a baby on my right hip and a glass of wine in my left hand. I felt so guilty, wondering if my daughter would walk in the door, scream at my derelict actions, grab the baby, and rush her to a child therapist. Then the chef offered me a sample of some warm rhubarb-strawberry pie with ice cream. Oh, my! How I needed that pie!

Only the purest organic food passes the lips of my gorgeous grandchild, but there I was sipping wine and spooning rhubarb and ice cream into her eager mouth. Such delight for both of us! It was so much better than all those fresh green beans and squash she eats! Grandma really knows how to have a good time.

I bundled her home and told her never to tell her mommy what we had done. After all, what happens with Tutu stays with Tutu.

Another time, one of my granddaughters spent the day with me, and we read books, emptied drawers, danced, crawled under tables, tumbled on the carpet, poked toys into little boxes, and played peek-a-boo with a silk blanket. I even introduced her to steamed cauliflower—so much better than the crap I used to feed my kids when they were small.

I'd forgotten how busy a toddler can be. In desperate need of a toilet, I took her into the bathroom with me, and it took only ten seconds for her to open drawers and find the razor blades. These were not on her mom's recommended toy list. Then she scampered away with a tube of lotion, which she quickly squirted onto my hardwood floor before I could get my pants zipped.

Just when I was ready to offer her a real pony if she took a nap, she got tired and we cuddled in the rocking chair. Then she fell asleep in her little crib, and I watched in amazement and relief as she sighed her way to some mysterious dreamland. After my wonderful, perfect daughter took my wonderful, perfect granddaughter back home, I poured a glass of Moon Mountain cabernet sauvignon and sat quietly to contemplate my blessings. Hey Diddle, Diddle, and the cow jumped over the Moon Mountain.

I'm often reminded that children are tiny bundles of magical power. My sweet granddaughter, Sweetie Pie, celebrated her birthday with a festive party as four generations enjoyed brunch and mimosas prepared by her parents, singing by her cousins, and a musical program from her grandparents.

The amazing reality of this event was that fifteen adults of totally diverse backgrounds and beliefs came together to celebrate this wonderful little girl. We had liberals, conservatives, agnostics, new-agers, a vegetarian, and a widow who still thinks Eisenhower is president. At least three guests own a concealed weapon permit, and several others wouldn't have a gun in the house. We represent a sample of America, and we'll probably cancel out one another's votes during the next presidential election.

But we came together to sing, laugh, and celebrate the extraordinary life of this little girl who learned to walk when she was three. Sweetie Pie was born with ten fingers, ten toes, and Down syndrome. And she has the power to unite all of us.

I've never been one to wallow on the "Life is not fair" pity party, but I was confused about the unknown: Why did this happen? How do we help? What is her future? What about my daughter?

Four years after the initial shock, the extended family now is convinced that this little bundle of funny faces, squawking noises, and death-grip hugs has much to teach us about love and life. And she answers my worried questions: It happened because an extra chromosome appeared in the early stages of fetal development. We can help by loving her and offering to help her parents. Her future is better than if she had been born fifty years ago and institutionalized. And her mother outshines Wonder Woman.

Uneducated and insecure people reveal their prejudices when they ridicule someone with Down syndrome. When I'm with Sweetie Pie, sometimes I get "the look of pity" from others or the recognizable sigh of "I'm thankful that didn't happen to me." Thanks to Sweetie Pie, I have learned that ignorance and cruelty are bigger handicaps than a little extra chromosome.

It's not all hugs and kisses. Sweetie Pie faces developmental challenges that other toddlers don't experience. She only recently learned to walk and has a limited vocabulary. Some children with Down syndrome require regular appointments with various specialists, and other siblings must adapt to the family's schedules. But Sweetie Pie was born with her parents' tenacity and her own unique strength. She is destined to amaze all of us.

We have a photograph of my daughter with her two daughters. She is holding her newborn baby who is wearing oxygen tubes as the three-year-old stands beside them. My daughter looks into the distance, and her gaze reflects all the emotions of a dedicated woman. I know she'll fight like a warrior to protect and raise her children, and with the help of a good husband, she is the strength, the passion, and the force that make everything work. She is awesome. Of course, she is. After all, she's my daughter.

～

Know Your Roots and Color
if Necessary

Wendell, Idaho is a small farming community in southern Idaho where you can get to Clell and Mabel's home by turning left at the brown house with the wooden deck, just past the hill by Chandler's dairy barn. I grew up there, as did my parents and a colorful assortment of relatives. Most have passed on, but I'll never forget their pioneer spirit.

"Quit daydreaming and go pick some peas!" The impatient and practical voices of my long-departed grandmothers echo in my ears when I fall into a pensive mood. Both were sturdy, stubborn farm women in southern Idaho who lived well into their nineties. They had calluses on their hands, lines on their faces, and a look in their eyes that declared, without a doubt, they could and would do anything to survive.

They didn't have time to pamper a worried granddaughter when there was a garden to weed, pigs to be fed, and the menfolk to please. I didn't inherit all of their traits! I agreed that weeding and feeding were important, but I stomped my saddle shoes at an early age and refused to wait on men as my grandmothers and mother obeyed and served their husbands. I believed then, as I do now, that an adult woman and man can please each other in significant and equal amounts ...with or without handcuffs.

Despite our differences in opinions, I respected my grandmothers for their strength and wisdom. Their vintage advice often boiled down to succinct admonishments:

- Tired of being tired? Get off your butt and go for a walk.

- Want more money? Spend less than you make.

- Want a special meal? Make it yourself.

- Still using a stapler to fix that loose hem? Learn how to mend it.

- Want steamy romance? Cook in your underwear.

- Want perfect children? Don't have any.

During my childhood, farm life was full of births, deaths, planting, and reaping. Every spring, the pastures were dotted with huddled clumps of new calves. Old hogs and new piglets that didn't survive would be stacked in a pile for the rendering man. The raw cycle of life was a true reality show, and I preferred to enjoy it from the back of my horse as I rode over the river and through the pastures to grandmother's house.

Grandma Olive, my mother's mom, had an efficient talent for killing chickens. A petite woman in her gingham dress and work apron, she looked like the picture on the cover of *Ladies' Home Journal*. But when it was time for a chicken dinner, she rolled up her sleeves, trotted out to the yard, grabbed a hapless fowl by the neck, and swung it around like a lasso. Then with a quick flick of her wrist, that poor chicken was as dead as a doorknob. And Grandma would stand there without a hair out of place or a speck of blood on her apron.

Sometimes, if company was coming and she was in a hurry, she'd grab two chickens and chop off their heads on the block by the coop. She'd have the feathers plucked off one chicken before the second one's headless body could flounder too far away. Those birds were gutted and in the oven in record time.

Grandma Clell, my paternal grandmother, always opened her home to weary travelers, visiting relatives, and runaway granddaughters. Though quite the hostess, she had rules that no one should stay longer than necessary. I have improvised some of those rules for myself when I have houseguests who don't want to leave:

- Take them to the airport early. Preferably two days before their flight.

- Cook naked.

- Have cockroach traps on the dining table.

- Hide a condom in their bed.

- Stock the guest bathroom with one Hello Kitty towel and four sheets of toilet paper.

- Loudly play polka music featuring the Six Fat Dutchmen.

- Serve burned toast and one sausage—for dinner.

- Host a meeting of your Toenail Biters Support Group, TBSG.

- Close your bedroom door and continually play the fake orgasm scene from *When Harry Met Sally.*

- Answer your cell phone, scream "Oh no!" and run out of the house.

- Buy several pairs of the biggest size of women's underwear you can find—and leave them drying on the couch.

- Show home movies of your colonoscopy.

My Cousin Lucille was a gracious and bodacious woman known for her wise predictions and prognostications. A well-endowed and well-meaning woman, she had seven children and breastfed each one for over a year. She'd go around the house doing chores with one hand while her other arm held a baby tucked under her blouse just grabbing on and smacking for dear life.

As a result of this maternal devotion, by age forty Cousin Lucille could tuck her pendulous mammary glands into her belt. She remedied this situation by ordering industrial-strength brassieres from the Sears and Roebuck catalog. The fabric was military-grade, and she would ratchet up the straps with a socket wrench until her chest resembled two large torpedoes that could go off at any minute and wipe out the barn.

The women of the Church Ladies of Gooding County often snickered behind Cousin Lucille's broad back. She didn't care. She always advised her children that before they judged someone, they should walk a mile in her shoes. "After that, who cares?" she'd say. "The mean person is a mile away, and you've got her shoes."

Ever a lady, Cousin Lucille was determined to hang on to what was left of her youth. She declared that gravity was the enemy and there were evil forces in the universe out to destroy our bodies and reduce them to quivering lumps of oozing fat. She defied the hands of time by fighting back with creams, lotions, and potions. She declared that she would not take old age lying down, unless of course, romance was in the air, and then, by all means, be grateful.

After the premature death of her husband, Uncle Lucky, Cousin Lucille devoted her life to getting her children out on their own so she could develop her consulting business. Her talent was to write and disseminate a regular list of predictions and prognostications that was published in the *Gooding County Gazette*. She did so after consulting lunar charts, scientific data, and a bottle of Jack Daniels. She divided her advice into helpful suggestions for each month.

Cousin Lucille's Helpful Hints
for Sassy Middle-Aged Women

- **January**—It's time to clean your house during the half-moon before the third week of the month. You'll find your cat that has been missing since October. To freshen musty air, set out an open dish of vinegar. For faster results, dip a towel in the vinegar and whirl it around. That's also a good exercise to prevent flabby arms.

- **February**—It's time to lose that winter malaise. Enroll in a yoga class, only if the instructor is a young athlete with bad eyesight. Ask him to manually adjust your Downward Facing Dog position. Repeat, if necessary.

- **March**—To defy the effects of gravity, practice standing on your head at regular intervals. For added delight, do this propped up against the washing machine during the spin cycle. Make sure the men and children are out of the house.

- **April**—Plan a new hobby or learn a new game to share with friends. But never play pool in a tight white skirt because when you lean over the table for a bank shot, your rear end will look like two dimpled pumpkins in a bag.

- **May**—Plant some petunias and mint so in the summer you can have flowers on the table and mint for your juleps. Then enjoy an early morning walk in the woods. And, if you get a tick, just cover that insect with some petroleum jelly. That will suffocate the varmint, and then you can unscrew it counterclockwise from your skin. Save dead ticks in a jar to add to casseroles you give to those who have done you wrong.

- **June**—It's time to prepare Drunken Fruit for Christmas! Pour a quart of rum into a sterile crock or jar. Add three cups of fresh, rinsed, whole fruit (peaches, cherries, strawberries, and/or apricots). Cover with a clean cloth, and store in a cool, dark spot for six months. Open the crock on Christmas Day, serve the fruit with the holiday meat, and sip your homemade brandy after dinner. It will make the in-laws seem so much more interesting, and by evening you'll all be singing your own version of the "Hallelujah Chorus."

- **July**—For a good patriotic exercise, stand up twenty times and salute the flag and shake your fists at anyone who doesn't. Just for fun, let the cows out and then chase them back into the pasture. You get to whoop and holler while getting some exercise.

- **August**—Stay out of the sun, or you'll look like luggage on legs. Forget those expensive face creams. Just use some light mineral oil and tissue off the excess. Use Vaseline or Bag Balm to heal and soothe chapped hands. It's also time to stock up on hemorrhoid ointment to reduce those unsightly, puffy bags under the eyes. To brighten tired eyes, heat two tea bags in two cups of water for five minutes. Lie down and cover your eyelids with the tea bags. Remember to cool the bags first, or you'll scald your eyeballs.

- **September**—It's time to dig some new potatoes and make a big pot of creamed spuds. Add a baked ham, some fresh beans, and warm apple crisp. Serve this to your man, and he'll reward you later with something even more steamy and delicious.

- **October**—All that harvest produce can make your breath smell like Old Man Bettencourt's pigpen on a hot day. For an effective mouthwash, mix ½ teaspoon each of borax and sodium bicarbonate with 4 teaspoons glycerin and 2/3 cup distilled water. Add 3 teaspoons of vodka for an extra-happy grin.

- **November**—It's time to give thanks for your blessings and that the banker's rich wife looks older than you do. Be extra grateful if your parents aged well, if your children love life, if you have at least one friend you can call any time, and if you can still slow dance an entire song in the arms of a lover. Preferably your lover.

- **December**—This is a good month to laugh, but be careful or you'll get those crinkly lines around your eyes, and a really good belly laugh could make you wet your pants. So could excess helpings of Drunken Fruit.

For many small country towns, a funeral was cause for considerable excitement and competition. It's always special when somebody dies because the anticipated funeral provides opportunities for the local women to show off their cooking skills. The Church Ladies Society always prepared meals for the bereaved families after the funeral, and the buffet often rivaled any food contest at the county fair. But the dignity of the event could be altered by friendly feuds at the funeral functions.

The humiliation of not having the most popular dish at the funeral dinner provided quite an incentive within the charitable women of the Church Ladies Society, and woe to the cook whose dish was not empty after the meal. Tables would be loaded with colorful Jell-O salads, chicken casseroles, buttered beans with fried onions, hot-cross buns, platters of vegetables garnished with radish roses, and plenty of pies and cakes.

One time, Matilda Teaberry, the president of the Society, brought a potato salad that was, bar none, the worst concoction and abuse of potatoes ever eaten by any suffering friends of any deceased person. As the dinner progressed, Matilda became more and more agitated as the other plates and bowls were scooped clean, and her salad remained uneaten, practically screaming, "Loser! Bad cook!"

The other members of the Society, ever polite and dignified, began to sneak large portions of the potato salad and quietly dump the foul mess into the garbage. Matilda was relieved when she saw that her salad had been the most popular one at the funeral dinner. So she continued to bring the salad to funerals for the next twenty years, and her loyal Society friends would take turns spooning and dumping it into the garbage. Small-town funerals prove how even ghastly potato salad can bring friends together in times of need for the betterment of society.

As a child, I relied on my wits to survive. I was the only girl in a hardworking farm family, and my importance fell way below that of my brothers, my mother, the hired hands, the dog, and the cats. The dog was useful for barking at strangers, and the cats were necessary to control the mice. The hired hands worked hard on my father's farms from sunrise until sunset.

My mother, bless her heart, dutifully had dinner on the table every night at six o'clock, whether or not my father came in from work. If he was late, she silently added more milk to the gravy and kept the pork chops in the oven until they became hard enough to use as doorstops. But just smother those chops with globs of reheated gravy, and you could choke 'em down with a few glasses of dairy-fresh milk.

My brothers were important, well, because they were male. It all seemed so unfair.

My grandmother's generic treatments for our childhood illnesses were successful because we were too terrified to get sick. The potions and homemade remedies combined country folklore with whatever magic medicine was stocked in the pantry. Only sissies and townsfolk went to the doctor.

Grandma's healing practices were legendary. If we had a sore throat, she would wrap raw bacon in a tea towel and pin it around our neck. Consequently, my brothers and I never mentioned if we felt sick. Suffering in silence was preferable to smelling like a meat locker.

Another home remedy for coughs was to smear Vicks VapoRub on the soles of our feet, cover them with thick stockings, and send us to bed. If that didn't work, we were fed raw onions and honey. Needless to say, we held back a cough until our ears bled.

The cure for earaches was practical. Heat a green onion in the stove and then stick it in the painful ear. The warm vegetable would dissolve any wax buildup and eliminate the pain. Just don't look in the mirror or answer the door while wearing onions in your ears.

One nifty trick to remove fish bones stuck in our throats was to swallow a raw egg. If that didn't absorb the irritating bones and flush them down, the thick substance caused us to vomit the bones and the egg. Mission accomplished.

I remember injuring my elbow after falling out of a tree. Grandma wrapped my arm in a tea towel made from a flour sack and tied the ends around my neck. I wasn't able to climb another tree for several years, and my arm is still crooked.

Back in those days, Grandma was under pressure to make do with what she had. She made soap, churned butter, sewed clothes for her children, and baked every meal from scratch. Her pantry held a cornucopia of canned fruits and vegetables. And remedies. But we all survived, healthy and happy.

One of the last memories of my Grandmother Olive is of her making dolls to sell at local craft sales. She was well into her eighties and lamenting that it took longer to make the clothes because her eyesight was failing. I visited with her one afternoon.

"Grandma, can I help?"

She sat in her favorite chair, surrounded by small tables heaped with plastic doll heads, stuffed cloth doll bodies, and sewing supplies. She was crocheting a dress for her latest creation.

"Yes, can you finish sewing on her head and dressing that doll for me? I think she would like the red and white one."

Of course my grandmother knew what outfit each doll would prefer. I made sure I had the head facing in the correct position and then struggled with the needle and thread until I stabbed my thumb, but there was only one drop of blood and I wiped it on my jeans. I would have sucked out all the blood from my arm rather than stain one of the plump bodies. I finished the head and then wiggled the red dress onto the doll and tied on the matching hat. I heard Grandma muttering.

"Is that okay?" I asked.

"No, she's not happy. Pull the hat back from her eyes so her face shows. She's so pretty."

I did as instructed and then turned to dress more dolls. As I carefully tied each hat, I talked with Grandma about her sewing skills. Her needles never stopped clicking and creating as she spoke.

"I made all of your mother's and your aunt's clothes. I didn't have patterns so I guessed how to cut the material. Daddy would give me the milk money to get material and I would buy bolts at a time. I used an old treadle sewing machine that still works. Your mother had the best dresses in school."

She smiled, stopped her handiwork, and closed her eyes.

"Are you alright, Grandma? Can I get you some tea?"

She rocked awhile without answering. Sunshine peeked through the lace curtains, fell over her plant stands laden with prized geraniums and violets, and then illuminated a face etched with character and experience. The clock on the wall continued to tick, and I began to worry.

Then she opened her eyes and sighed.

"We can finish five more dolls today. Then it's time for some apple pie. You like apple pie, don't you?"

"Only if it's yours."

She squinted and looked at me through her eyeglasses.

"I've always been so shy. You've always been so, well, so loud. And you make people laugh."

I was going to apologize but she held up a wrinkled hand.

"Don't change," she said. "I suppose it's good to laugh."

That was our last conversation.

Sometimes in her honor and to consume generous portions of fruit and calcium, I eat a warm apple pie with lots of ice cream. That's the least I can do to preserve the precious memories.

$\sim$

23770455R00126

Made in the USA
Middletown, DE
02 September 2015